STUDENT BODY SHOTS - ANOTHER ROUND

Max —
Enjoy teaching
people to not
be like me.

Plan:
Enjoy teaching.
people to act
be like me.

STUDENT BODY SHOTS - ANOTHER ROUND

more sarcasm on the best four to six years of your life

STEVE HOFSTETTER

Independent Books for Independent Readers

Student Body Shots - Another Round © 2005 Steve Hofstetter

Cover Designer: Barbara Hodge
Interior Design: Mary Jo Zazueta

All rights reserved. No part of this book may be reproduced, stored in a retrieval system, or transmitted in any form by any means electronic, mechanical, photocopying, recording, or otherwise except in brief extracts for the purpose of review, without the permission of the publisher and copyright owner.

ISBN: 1-59411-123-5

Library of Congress Control Number: 2004098290

Printed in the United States of America

10 9 8 7 6 5 4 3 2 1

Published by The Writers' Collective ▲ Cranston, Rhode Island

*This book is dedicated to Dad
He wants so much for the world
to learn how to spell "Hofstetter"*

Contents

Foreword	*ix*
Acknowledgments	*xi*
Welcome to College	1
The Daily Grind	9
Pieces of the Puzzle	25
The Social Life	35
Men and Women	47
Academics	53
The Supporting Cast	63
Facilities	77
Holidays and Events	83
The End	97

The Foreword/Forward

I must admit this is the first time I've ever been asked to write a foreword to a book, and I'll confess it makes me feel guilty for rarely reading forewords, and never with my full attention. And since I rarely read them, I'm really not all that certain on how to write one.

Webster's Dictionary defines "Forward" as: Toward a place in front, onward; ready, bold, pert; advanced beyond the usual degree. Yes, that's me—ready, bold, pert. And since I went to five different universities for almost nine years, my degree should be considered advanced. (Every summer my life would spin off in a new direction, resulting in seven different majors. I ended up being a double-major; Law and Psychology. I figured I could be an asshole and know why.)

Although I don't know much about writing a foreword, I do know why Steve asked me to write it. Three times I have been voted either "Campus Comic Of The Year" or "Campus Performer Of The Year." I've spent almost a decade performing at over five hundred colleges, covering all fifty states. If you are a college student reading this, chances are I'll be at your school before you graduate. In fact, it's safe to say I spend more time on campus now than when I was actually enrolled in college.

Being on tour forty weeks a year, every year, I have discovered that almost every city has cool offbeat places the Chamber of Commerce won't tell you about. You can only find out about these hidden treasures from someone who has "been there, done that." This book does the same for the college experience—tells you all the cool stuff that the administration won't. Before reading this, I thought there were only two universal truths about college life: there's no parking, and dorm food sucks. But you hold in your hands a virtual wealth of insights to college survival that would take years to learn on your own (nine, in my case.)

If you purchased this book because you are making the transition from high school to college, you made a wise choice. Twelve dollars is a small price to pay for the knowledge these pages contain. Sure, to put it in college terms, twelve bucks would buy enough ramen noodles to build a house (but, as a comedian friend of mine pointed out, when it rained the house would get really big).

So I encourage you to enjoy the faux pearls of wisdom in this book. This will probably be the last book you'll read for pleasure in the next four years (or nine, in my case.)

OK, I'm finished. Hope that was ready, bold, and pert enough for you.

– Spanky
Campus Activities Today Magazine
Readers' Choice Campus Comic of the Year

Acknowledgments

I thank the following people for the role they have played in this book, and in my life in general.

Rick Van Veen, Josh Abramson, Jakob Lodwick, Zach Klein, Julie Kraut, and the rest of the CollegeHumor.com staff for all of their help in everything one more time. Josh Jacobs for the ultimate road trip. Spanky, Matt Boor, Court Sullivan, Ben Applebaum, and Ari Stern for their contributions to both this book and my daily entertainment. Cahill for the title (still). My readers for that whole "audience" thing. All the organizations that brought me to campus especially the Columbia University Bookstore and the Meredith Entertainment Association. Danny McDermott for my start in stand-up. Eddie Ifft, Pete Dominick, Lenny Marcus, Ben Morrison, and all the Comedy *Soapbo*x comedians. John, Phil, JP, Rory, and everyone else at Sirius. My family for their surprisingly continued willingness to put up with me. SigEp for being my extended family. And everyone else who helped *Student Body Shots* become the fun, educational, and wild ride it's been.

Chapter 1

Welcome to College

And we're back. I know what you're thinking: how could this guy possibly have anything more to say about college life? And why should I give him another twelve bucks to do it? Well, I've spent the last two years talking to college newspapers, traveling to different campuses, and seeing what's out there, and the main thing I've learned is that freshmen think I'm sketchy. But the other lesson is that I haven't yet made fun of half the crap that goes on in school. There's a lot out there—so much that I may even do a third book (cough cough).

As you begin your journey through these pages, approach it with the same mentality as you would college. There are passages meant to teach you a few things (like some classes), and there are also passages that offer no educational value (like some classes). Some of the book is informative (unlike your friend's notes), some of the book is entertaining (unlike a capella groups), and some of the book is great at football (unlike my school's team). OK, this book doesn't play football, but I had to get that jab in there somehow.

You do not have to have read the first *Student Body Shots* to enjoy *Another Round*. But if you'd like to read the original book before continuing with the sequel, you can put this one down for now. Like your parents after you graduate and can't find a job, we'll be there when you come back.

And like I said before: welcome to college.

Finishing High School

You will never have less responsibility than you do the final few weeks of high school. You have no more exams, your teachers don't care if you go to class or not, and your parents still cook and clean for you. And if you manage to mess anything up, screw it—you're leaving town in three months.

Remember how expensive prom night seemed? It cost $100 to rent a tux, $150 for your share of the limo, $20 for the alcohol you snuck in before it got confiscated, and another $30 for the new alcohol you bought later that night. It came to $300, but it paid for what could be one of the most memorable nights in your entire life. Four months later, you spend close to that much on your calculus book.

The night after high school graduation, you feel more important than you ever have. You've finally accomplished what you've been working toward your whole life, and you just sit there on the top of the world. Savor it, because it will be the last time you're cool for a year and a half.

Some people skip their senior year of high school to go to college early. Sure, college is more fun than high school.

But senior year is the best year of high school, and freshman year is the worst year of college. Especially if you're only seventeen.

If you want to look really smart, sign everyone's high school year book with "In three years, you'll barely remember what I look like." You may be a jerk for doing it, but man you'll be right.

Choosing Schools

This book is not going to accurately tell you which school to attend. Then again, neither will any of those $50 college guides.

They let you shop around for classes once you get to college, but not while you're choosing schools. The second half of your senior year of high school should be divided into two weeks spent at each campus you're considering. If you only got in to one or two schools, then you'd get a really long nap.

If they have career aptitude tests, why not college aptitude tests? And make them really comprehensive. That way you'll know where you should go to school, what to study when you get there, and who on your floor you're going to hook up with during orientation week.

Some parents get really involved in the college process, buying all the books, reading all the articles, and arranging all the tours. These are also the parents who've turned your room into a den by Columbus Day.

A lot of people go to school in-state because it's cheaper. Not only the tuition, but you save $5 a month by bringing your laundry home.

I almost went to school in Syracuse. I don't know how my life would have been different, but it certainly would have been colder.

Visiting a college is not like being a student there. Especially if your parents are with you.

Moving In

No matter how little stuff you think you're bringing with you, whoever is on the passenger side of the car ends up holding something on their lap while ducking to avoid whatever is jutting out from the back seat.

Every floor has one or two people adept at spatial relations who can arrange their furniture perfectly. But our dorms have been open for decades—you'd think there'd be set solutions for each room by now. When you move in, you should get a book of possible floor plans to at least give you an idea.

Almost every campus has the same policy when it comes to dealing with returning students on move-in day. Though "Screw 'em!" is more of a motto than a policy.

Guards on move-in day usually give you more attitude than normal. But that's because it's their busiest time of the year. Sitting behind a desk all day, signing people in is one thing, but to do it while watching kids carry everything they own up the stairs because the administration doesn't understand the idea of an express elevator? Man, that's just exhausting.

If you've never been to Boston on September 1st, I recommend it. Just don't do it in a U-Haul.

A lot of schools have orientation staff to help you move in. But all they do is wait with you in line and point you toward the elevator. When you've got everything you own sitting in two rolly carts, finding the elevator is not the help you need.

Orientation

I make a lot of jokes about how useless orientation week is. There's no punchline here, I'm just pointing it out.

How much better would it be if orientation packets came with the names, phone numbers, and menus of all the nearby takeout places?

I know the administration screens orientation leaders heavily, but they don't always do it correctly. The first question on every orientation advisor application should read, "Have you been holed up in the school library for the last two years? If you checked yes, please return this form to our office immediately, and try to remember where you last saw your life before you misplaced it."

The only thing sadder than a sophomore guy at an orientation dance is the freshman girl looking at him going, "Ooh, sophomore."

Some orientation activities seem out of place. I understand why they do name games and other such ice breakers, no matter how lame they end up being. But how is playing laser tag going to teach me about college?

My senior year, I volunteered to help with one of our orientation programs. My involvement let me move in a week early in exchange for only one hour of my time. And the first lesson I taught the freshmen was how to move in a week early in exchange for only one hour of their time.

Meeting People

I try not to ask someone's name the first time I meet them. Because if I don't know it, I can't be blamed for forgetting it.

First impressions are always either dead on or completely wrong. Three months later, you never sit there and say, "You know, I was very intermediate in how I felt about him."

It is way too easy to meet people in school. When you walk to class and you bump in to someone, you've made a new friend. Not right then—but so many of us stay on such strict schedules that you'll probably walk into the same person every week from then on.

The easiest time of year to meet a girl is not the beginning of the semester—it's actually the end. About a week before formal.

Right after you graduate college, there are many fewer people to meet, but they're a lot more eager to meet you. Because after the first week of school, everyone realizes that they can meet someone new whenever the heck they want. After the first week of work, everyone realizes that they can only meet someone new whenever they get fired and get a new job.

You don't realize how easy it was to meet people while you were in school until after you've already graduated. You get an apartment, and you wonder what's up all your neighbors' butts preventing them from coming over and saying hi. And then you're like, "Oh, right—lives."

First Week of School

By the end of the summer, your prevailing thought is about getting back to school. You miss your friends, you miss your ethernet, and you miss your freedom. So you get there, and you sit in class that first week, and your prevailing thought finally changes. Now it's: "What the hell was I thinking?"

You're given the same amount of work during the first week of school as you're given during any other week. But it seems like less because you don't yet have a backlog from all those weeks of work you've been ignoring.

The professors who don't let you into their classes when you miss the first day are ridiculous. You can miss all of November and still pass, but if you don't hear them read the syllabus aloud, you're never going to be able to catch up.

Why don't schools save professors some time and preprint index cards with blanks for your name, major, and year? Or just give professors a record of who is actually in their classes?

In high school, you dreaded the first week. But in college, you don't wake up early, you don't come home to your parents, and you live in a neighborhood full of people your own age. But you still have homework, so it balances out.

If you think students dread work the first week of school, consider the professors. They actually have to do the reading.

Chapter 2

The Daily Grind

There are approximately 2,500 colleges in the United States that have an enrollment greater than 1,000, and these schools have a lot of differences. Some rely on dorms, some on commuters. Some have semesters, some have trimesters, some have quarters, and some have no split at all. Some are two-year, some are four-year, and some are five-year—on purpose. Some have Greek life, some do not, and some have those Greek-lettered honor societies that are cheap knock-offs of Phi Beta Kappa. But every last one of them has one guy who asks way too many questions in class.

My point is that the big picture can be unique, but we share the details. An engineer and a history major can bond over how much homework they have hanging over them, despite not being able to understand each other's assignments. Our common experiences add up to make college a common experience, where everyone shares some level of understanding. And the scars to prove it.

I am a Jewish kid from New York, educated at a private university in the biggest city in the country. What if you're of a different religion, grew up on a farm, and went to a rural state school? Does that mean that your shower shoes traipsed through any less fungus, or that your ATM's lack of tens is any less annoying? No—that stuff makes up the daily grind and happens to everyone. Hopefully more often to that kid who asks *way* too many questions.

Sleep

So it turns out that if you get more than three hours of sleep on a weeknight, you don't need fourteen hours on a weekend.

Cell phones should turn their ringers to vibrate automatically when they're not touched for more than three hours. Because if you leave your phone on just once, that will be the Tuesday night that your ex calls at 4 AM "needing to talk."

It's not easy for a guy to stay asleep when there's a girl in his bed with him. But it's incredibly easy for him to fall asleep in the first place.

It's impossible to fall asleep when you need to. You can't sleep when you're consciously thinking about something, and when you need to fall asleep, all you can do is consciously think about how much sleep you're losing.

Life would be much easier if you could save up sleep. I'd have slept right through eighth grade and added an extra year of productivity to my life.

Falling asleep is the universal signal for "It's the right time to bang on my door asking for beer."

Imagine how much more productive we'd be if we didn't sleep. And how much uglier, too.

If you want to freak someone out when they wake you up, tell them that if you don't get your twenty-three and a half hours, you get really cranky.

Showers

Communal showers prepare you for life after college. The first place I lived after school was a house with four other guys, all a few years older than me, and they kept talking about how nasty our shower was getting. And every time I went in there, I couldn't figure out what they meant.

Why do some college bathrooms have those little cubbies for people's stuff? It is unsafe to leave anything there unguarded, and we all know it. Putting those shelves in is like having a sign at the bank asking you to please turn your back to the ATM during each withdrawal.

If I notice that a floormate hasn't showered in a few days, I usually keep it to myself. But the second he brags about it, it's out of my hands.

College bathrooms can be notorious for how cold they get during the winter. The windows have virtually no insulation, and you'd be better off heating the place with a toaster oven than the 40-year-old radiators in there. Yet the bathroom is really where heat is most important. The only time I'm ever cold and wet in my room is after I run screaming from the shower because it's so damn cold.

Sure, it costs colleges money to have good water pressure in the shower. But if they do, students will be more refreshed, thus get better grades, thus get better jobs, thus earn more money, and thus donate more to the school. So fix our showers—you're only hurting yourself.

Clothes

Everyone has their own style in college. Especially weird kids who dress funny.

When you have a favorite jacket, you don't start wearing it the first day it gets cold—you start wearing it the first day it gets cold-er. 80 degrees in July? Perfect for a black leather jacket.

How come the girl who gets all hooched out for class is the same girl who ignores the guy next to her?

Nothing commemorates a college event better than a gigantic ugly logo on an otherwise nice T-shirt.

If you have a few retro T-shirts, that's cool. If your whole wardrobe is a tribute to Olivia Newton John, the cool wears off after a while.

I've gotten into the habit of actually telling girls when I think they look good in something that they're wearing because I know that girls appreciate that kind of stuff. But I am very careful not to get too specific. It's not polite to say, "You know, your breasts look really good in that."

My friend used to wear a Cornell shirt around Columbia, and people would give him weird looks. One kid even said, "but you go to Columbia!" And that's exactly why he didn't need a shirt saying it.

Unless you slept in that dirty T-shirt and pajama pants, you're not allowed to wear them to class. It's just as easy to open a closet as it is to open the hamper.

Television

If you don't have a TV set one year, you'll love the freedom it gives you. Then you end up with one the next year, and wonder why you ever cared about freedom when you could have had SportsCenter.

The Nielson's are a flawed system. *Sex and the City* would have a much higher rating if you could count all of the times college girls packed a room ten deep to watch the show.

Every time someone comes along and tries to create a national college cable network, they market shows produced solely by college students. Why? We may be in college, but we like good TV like anyone else. No one ever thinks that plumbers prefer shows made by other plumbers.

There's more and more of a trend to put celebrities in reality TV shows. You know why? Because we're starting to slowly understand that real people's lives are just as boring as, well, ours.

A lot of times, a commercial tells me that if I see only one episode of their show this season, it's got to be this one. The FCC really needs to make sure they're only saying that once a season, or we'll all wind up very confused.

Your standards get so much lower when you don't have cable. It's like being at a bar at the end of the night. "Well, I already saw this movie a few times, but this other channel doesn't look so great and hey—I gotta watch something."

Movies

Watching action movies, I've learned that good guys always win because bad guys are stupid. Watching real life, bad guys can be pretty freakin' smart.

When colleges show movies, they usually show something that all the students have seen a hundred times. And that's exactly what we want. Because going to a movie with a bunch of your friends is less about seeing something good, and more about seeing who remembers more of the lines.

Do not rent a movie on a date if your DVD player is on your computer. It is not romantic to pull two chairs up to a desk and squint.

The younger you are, the less likely it is that you've already become jaded. So when you're in college, there are still a lot of kids around convinced that they're going to make it as actors. I tossed around the idea of writing a screenplay, and I already have seventy-three people starring in it.

I was so excited when I found out I could download movies off of the campus network that I grabbed anything I could get my hands on. A few months later, I was flipping through my CDs and saw *The Santa Clause*, *George of the Jungle*, and *Troll 2*. Thanks, ethernet.

You need a VCR or a DVD player when you're in school, even if you hate watching TV. There will be a point in time when you want the option of saying, "We could just go back to my room and watch a movie."

Breakfast

College students eat breakfast much more often than most people give us credit for. Right before we go to sleep.

I have a tradition where I make myself a nice breakfast the first morning of every semester. Eggs, home fries, toast, orange juice—it's a nice way of telling myself, "Hey buddy, it'll be six months before you have the motivation to do this again."

Bars close later in New York City than most other places. Yet college breakfast curiously starts at the same time everywhere. Your last call and your first cup of coffee are related much more closely than the administration realizes.

I don't understand people who never eat breakfast. Some days, being hungry is the only thing that wakes me up.

Why are there breakfast meats but no dinner cereals? Forget that—why are there breakfast meats in the first place?

If you're a big cereal eater, you run out of milk often. If you're a big cereal eater with roommates, you don't know you've run out of milk until after you've filled your bowl with cereal.

There is a place near my campus that only serves hash browns from 7:00 to 8:00 in the morning. Which sucks, because that's the one hour that I don't see from either side.

Lunch

In high school, you scheduled an hour break to get something to eat, and that was plenty of time because you already had lunch with you, or you bought your lunch locally. But in college, you usually spend your own money, and campus is much more spread out. Even if you want to save cash by making ramen or macaroni and cheese, you still have to go home, make it, eat it, and get to your next class—which usually takes more than an hour. So you've either got to skip lunch, schedule a two-hour long break in the middle of the day, or just start your whole day later, shifting every meal down one. And then you need to schedule time between classes to eat dinner.

Having the dining hall open in the morning but not in the afternoon is like closing up your lemonade stand when the sun comes out.

Girls: When a guy asks to buy you lunch, he wants to ask you to dinner and is slowly working up the nerve. When he asks you to buy him lunch, he wants to ask you to watch a movie in his room, but is slowly waiting until you're drunk.

One of my friends who worked in finance for the summer told me that he could never meet for lunch because he had to eat at his desk. Sure, he could IM and play flash minigolf while he ate there, but getting up was out of the question.

Is lunch the name for the second meal you eat or the name of the meal you eat between noon and two? Because in college, that is not the same thing.

Dinner

It's a cool idea to get a few friends together and rotate cooking every night. It's a cooler idea to actually follow through the rotation more than once.

The phrase, "Man, the food here sucks!" doesn't carry much weight when it's muffled by a mouth full of seconds.

College students would cook and eat together if we had a place to do it. But when your dining room table is an upside-down TV box, eating take-out Chinese in the lounge sounds like a pretty good idea.

There's almost always a really expensive restaurant right near campus. They should all have signs in the window that say, "We accept Visa, MasterCard, American Express, and your parents' money, because those are the only ways you're ever going to eat here."

Why do restaurants charge more for the same sized portions if it's later in the day?

People are surprised when I tell them I know how to cook well. But that's because everyone has a different definition of "well." I can't prepare dishes with names or anything. But give me ten bucks worth of pasta, vegetables, and chicken, and I can make a different dish every night for a week.

Freshmen: collect all the menus that delivery guys leave in your lobby for the next few years. Then right before graduation, walk into each restaurant, drop a pile on their floor, and say, "Same to you, buddy!"

Money

The big joke is that college students are constantly broke, right? Yet somehow, we're still the desired demographic for almost every product on the market today. I guess they figure if you can sell something to a broke-ass college student, then you can sell it to anyone.

If it weren't for eBay, the last week of college would be one giant yard sale.

If anyone whose parents pay for their tuition complains about being poor, they should be taken outside and shot.

No matter how little flexible income you may have, you already make over $30,000 a year more than I do.

People sit in Starbucks for hours at a time working on their laptops while drinking $7 coffee. How can people who do nothing all day afford that stuff? If you sit there long enough, someone must drop a bucket of money on your head.

I graduated at a really bad time for the economy. In a recession this deep, no one wants to pay someone fifty grand a year to slack off by forwarding funny e-mails and web sites to his friends. Which is unfortunate, because I'm really good at that.

After college, you get this urge to pay for stuff whenever you visit. "Hey," you say, "I'm working now, I got it." Which would make sense, except that you're not even making half of what you owe in student loans, and the people at the other end of the table are still living off of their parents.

E-mail

Why do some colleges complicate things when it comes to e-mail addresses? Give me my first name, my last name and an underscore, a hyphen, or a period. I can't think of a situation where I'd need to know that I'm the seventeenth guy with my initials to go to this school.

Some colleges are more tech savvy than others. Not the ones with really good e-mail systems—I mean the ones with really good domain names. The University of Colorado got cu.edu before Cornell, Columbia, and a billion other schools with those same initials. And University of Colorado shouldn't even be abbreviated CU. But the University of Cincinnati got to UC before they could.

I love that you can't use most versions of MS Outlook to check your Hotmail address. It was pretty bad when the Microsoft products weren't compatible with the rest of your software. Now they're even pissing off each other.

Three days after I graduated, my school took me out of the e-mail system. They had just enough time to send me a big fat donation request before they shut off my account.

If you go to a good school, you probably love giving out your e-mail address because it makes you sound all educated. Until you graduate, and you go from being the smartest guy in your neighborhood to being the loser who won't move on after college. "You can reach me by e-mailing i_dont_seem_to@have_a_life.edu."

Computers

You can no longer get by in school with an old computer. Sure, you say you only need a word processor and a web browser to survive, but that's because you don't yet know how to download all those movies off the network.

Now, home broadband is fairly common. But if you graduated a few years ago and moved to dial up, that was a pretty tough transition. You don't fly first class if you know you'll be in cargo for the rest of your life.

I don't want to know how people handled college before computers. I want to know how they handled college before Google.

My dad once told me a story about having to retype a paper the night before it was due, and his typewriter ribbon running out of ink. I came so close to saying, "Why didn't you just print it out in the lab?"

At my school, we're allowed to print 100 pages a week from the computer labs, so whenever anyone needs blank paper, they just make a blank 100-page document and print it out. I think it might be easier just printing 100 copies of one blank page, but I'm resourceful enough to buy my own one-cent paper, so what do I know?

Computers usually become obsolete within about two years, and definitely within three. Which is unfortunate, because some people get a computer freshman year and try to push it till graduation. And nothing helps a thesis along like a computer that won't turn on.

Phones

I once asked a friend of mine what we did about going out before we all had cell phones. He laughed before saying, "Made plans."

Why do I need a cell phone that lets me play video games? Don't they know I can already do that on my PDA?

When videophones first came out, no one got them because they cost about $3,000. Now they're cheaper than some cell phones, and no one has them anyway. I think we're all still scared of Mr. Spacely catching us sleeping.

A lot of phones have that same recording—a woman saying, "to leave a message, press one. For more options, press two." I appreciate the help and all, but the only option I really want to have beyond leaving a message is not leaving a message. That, I can do on my own.

Whoever said "Talk is cheap" never dialed a 976 number.

It's so much fun to watch someone who doesn't have a cell phone try to use yours. "Do I have to dial one? And the area code? Then what do I press? Send? Where is the Send button? The Okay button works, too? Then what do I do? Just talk?" And every time, they give the phone back to you without hanging up. I've finally learned to take off my keyguard before I hand the phone to one of these people because I don't like to see my friends cry.

Mail

I know that UPS coordinating the delivery of millions of packages is a difficult task, but there have been more than a dozen times when I've gotten the little yellow "you weren't there" slip even though I know I was home the whole day. Dude, you're already here, and that box isn't light. Ring my doorbell and save us both some trouble.

Our college mailrooms may serve half the people of a regular post office, but they try to do it with one-tenth the staff.

College mailboxes are tiny. Some of them, diagonally, are the exact width of a standard size envelope. Which would work perfectly if no one ever got more than one letter in a day.

The line to the mailroom is always twice as long as there are minutes until your next class.

Getting a package slip is regarded as wonderful, but only if it turns out to be a good package. Every once in a while you get there, and it's just an oversized sweepstakes envelope that couldn't fit into your mailbox.

The last few years I was at school, I lived off campus so I rarely checked my on-campus mail. After I graduated, I stopped by my mailbox on a whim and opened it, expecting to find a billion flyers from events I'd ignored. Instead, I found one letter telling me that I had the option to sign up to get letters about campus events. So I did.

Instant Messenger

I find myself compulsively trying to be creative in my away messages. At first it worked. And every once in a while, I still come up with a gem. But most of the time, it's a variation on "desperately trying to think of something creative."

Away messages are the one place where it's OK to quote yourself.

I have IMChaos all over my profile, and it helps me see who is checking out my stuff, and better yet, who knows my screen name. But what I love most about it are the times that my friends tell me they didn't click on a link because they didn't want to get caught looking at my profile. Dude, you just told me you read my profile. What's wrong with putting it in writing?

DSL did not catch on because people wanted high-speed connections at home. DSL caught on because people graduated but still wanted instant messenger on all day.

I have a rule—one person, one screen name. Giving me two screennames to add to my buddy list is like telling me two cell phone numbers. Not only will I not call both, I will not call either.

I should make a separate buddy category and call it, "People I will talk to only if no one else is online."

I know people who spend fifteen minutes every day going down their buddy list and reading all the away messages. I call these people "everyone."

Five Instant Away Messages (as if this entire book isn't made up of them)

5. How come you never call my phone to see if *that* message is creative?

4. Still angry at myself for wasting all that time clicking my friend's "drink beer" buddy icon as if it were a viable option. That's a weekend I'll never get back.

3. How many versions is it going to take before they give that poor yellow eunuch an IM Woman?

2. I was sitting around trying to come up with a good away message, and I couldn't. So I asked my roommate, and he IMed back that he was too busy. So I tried a few of my friends, and they couldn't think of anything, but we at least enjoyed the chat. I tried looking for one online, like a quote or something, and nothing stood out. And then finally it hit me: I am a loser. And I'm away.

1. I'm not touching you! I'm not touching you!

Music

Sometimes, schools put on festivals where they invite all the college bands to play, and then they advertise it like that's going to get you to come out. Every college has one, maybe two decent bands. Thanks for making me sit through eleven renditions of "Stairway" while I wait for them.

It's OK to love a local band. It's not OK to wonder why your friend who goes to school across the country has never heard of them.

Every college band has the same thing at all their shows: four of their friends, rocking out in the front, while the rest of the room says, "Who are these guys?" before turning back around and ordering another beer.

Every crappy, trying-to-make-it band has stickers made up. Have they ever thought of trying something that works instead?

It's good that the music industry got rid of free Napster. Because now when you use Morpheus, Limewire, Kazaa, or the billion other Napster clones, you're also supporting online gambling and internet porn.

Half the time you download a song off a network, it's just a local band who tried to get noticed by calling their filename something else.

It's ridiculous when someone in college tries to impress people by knowing someone in a band. Half the people in your school know someone in a band. And the other half are in bands.

Chapter 3

Pieces of the Puzzle

In the first book, I wrote about college as a puzzle, and took solace in the idea that there was a definite solution. When I graduated, my pieces were still strewn all over my floor, so I can't tell you whether or not I was right. Especially because I couldn't see them under all that laundry.

Perhaps college is a puzzle—but not a jigsaw puzzle. It might be a crossword or a word search or a jumble, or maybe even one of those random games that you find in the back of that puzzle book you bought to pass the time on an airplane. I hope not, because those games are so arbitrary that the only way to win is to cheat and look at the answers. Perhaps that is what you're doing by reading this book. Here's a tip: if you try to get through your own college experience based solely on what is in this book, your puzzle is going to wind up with a few extra letters. They will be "F" and "U" and they will be directed squarely at "I."

Whatever you decide your college experience most resembles, getting through it alive requires some problem-solving skills. Like Risk ("You know what the odds of you getting pregnant are?"), Taboo ("There's no way that girl is his sister."), and Chutes and Ladders ("This will be the best twelve-story beerbong ever!").

Before you go to school, think about whether you were the person with a hotel on Park Place or the poor sap in jail. Because college is a lot more fun if you understand how to win. Not like Jenga. That game sucks either way.

Sports

College athletes may not be paid in cash, but they're paid in beer and play. And giving a college student beer and play is like giving a prison inmate a truckload of cigarettes. It may not be government-backed currency, but it's worth a hell of lot more where you are.

A friend of mine went to the University of Alabama, and she said that everyone goes home on weekends when there are no football games. How is this possible? First of all, what do you do for fun when the season ends? Second of all, what do you do for fun on a Wednesday?

The problem with going to school in New York is that every school has tons of alumni here. And that sucks for our sports teams, because even home games are away games. Nothing makes a Columbia player prouder than looking up into the stands and hearing, "Go Dartmouth!"

It's shocking to me that college football still doesn't have a playoff system. You know why? They're worried that it will devalue the current bowl series that is already in place. Yeah, because college basketball's playoff system doesn't generate that much interest. And I can't remember the last time my friends and I missed the GalleryFurniture.com Bowl.

If you have three college friends come over to your suite to watch the Super Bowl, please do not refer to it as a party. Regardless of whether or not you have a bowl of nachos.

Laundry

No one likes to do laundry because it takes so much time. But when you think about it, a load of laundry only takes about twenty minutes of your time. It's three minutes to put it in, two minutes to move it to the dryer, and fifteen minutes to fold it and put it away. You'll wait on line to get into a bar for a half hour, but you won't spend twenty minutes making sure you have something to wear while you're there.

I learned quickly not to put laundry detergent directly on anything other than boxers or white T-shirts. College has too many black-light parties to let me make that mistake again.

I do laundry when I'm down to my worst pair of jeans. I don't wear them while I do laundry because they're my worst pair; they're my worst pair because I wear them while I do laundry. I'll put it this way—you can't wash 'em while you're still in 'em.

I have a hooded sweatshirt that I've never washed, and somehow it has no stains at all. But every time I wear a tuxedo, I come out looking like Jackson Pollack.

There was a scandal at Boston College where someone was running around stealing women's underwear. I'm glad they caught the guy, but who the hell is going to do something about the clown that's been snatching all of our socks?

If you live in a place with your own washing machine and dryer after you graduate, it's a weird adjustment. It'll be three months before you stop hoarding quarters.

Cold Weather
The first time you have to remember to bring a pair of gloves with you is really tough. You may not even wear them for the first few weeks they're in your pockets, but just knowing that they're there makes you instantly colder.

Really big coats and extra-thick sweaters were designed so that girls with nippleitis wouldn't be embarrassed as often.

Whenever I come in out of the rain, my jacket soaking, my hair dripping, and my pants with those little wet blotches all over them, someone always asks the same question: "Is it still raining?"

The first time you have to wear gloves isn't so cold. The first time you have to wear them to sleep? Now that's cold.

I used to be nervous about wearing my leather jacket in the rain. But the cows are OK, so why should I be any different?

Playing in the snow is not nearly as much fun as it was when we were younger. You know, like when we were freshmen.

The first day it gets cold, and I mean scarf-wearing, head-shivering, bone-chilling cold, you think, "My god, how am I ever going to get through this horrible day?" And that's about three seconds before you realize that you are the warmest you will be for the next three months.

Warm Weather

How happy do you get that first warm day of the year? You just walk around, and the whole time you don't care that you've just tanked a midterm, you locked your key in your room and you are completely broke, because hey—sun.

I don't know what it is about them, but after you wear shorts the first time it's almost impossible to switch back to jeans.

I like warm weather because people wear less, and the human body is a beautiful thing. Well, every once in a while.

I could never go to school in San Diego. I don't want to get pissed when the temperature drops all the way down to sixty-five.

It's hard to sleep when your room is really hot. Unless you're supposed to wake up for class. Then sleep is easy.

Skinny people don't favor warm weather because it helps us show off our bodies. We like it because cold weather really sucks when you have no body fat to keep you warm.

Do not try to pass off your shower shoes as sandals once it gets warm, even if they started out as sandals. Once they enter the shower with you, they become shower shoes. And if you wear shower shoes outside, God will tell you to take them off before you track shower room all over his dirt.

Being Sick

When you're sick, you're the most important person in the world. You don't care what other people say, do, or think as long as it doesn't impede your being as comfortable as possible. Whatever controls your body temperature must be somehow tied to your willingness to sacrifice for others.

I wonder if my professors get as excited about me being out sick as I get when it happens to them.

Why is it that your mother knows exactly what to do for every type of sickness you could get? I understand this when someone has a lot of kids. But when you're an only child and you come down with something you've never had before, how the heck does your mom know how to get you over it? And why is it always based on the color of your crap?

People develop preferences for cold medicine by taking the first thing that worked and using it for the rest of their lives. I doubt anyone sick is comparing two cold medicines at the register and thinking, "Well, dith thuff hepped lath dime, bud I wadda thee if dith dew thuff workth beddah."

I don't care who you are—if you're sick, chicken soup will help. Except if you're a chicken. Then that's kind of nasty.

When you're sick, there are two outlooks. Either you say, "If I make it through today, I'll feel better tomorrow," or you say "My god, I'm never going to feel better." Either way, today pretty much sucks.

Planes

College students have a ton of different frequent flyer numbers, because we take the cheapest flight, no matter what the airline. Then it's fun to get our statements every month telling us that with just 24,400 more frequent flyer miles, we could actually earn something.

A lot of airlines don't serve peanuts anymore, and give us pretzels instead. But they still haven't grasped the whole "save the salty food until after they already have drinks" concept.

I love the people on planes that order a mini Jack and Coke and act like it's got enough liquor to calm them down. If my tolerance were so low that one of those drinks did the trick, I'd have to avoid rum cake entirely.

Sometimes, when I'm bored on an airplane, I try to imagine what I'd do if the whole thing got hijacked. And I always envision myself saving the day. I wonder if anyone's out there picturing how they'd wet their pants and then get themselves shot for crying too much.

If cell phones really made planes crash, wouldn't terrorists have grasped this by now? There'd be twelve guys lining the aisles with Nokias, threatening to hit "Send."

Sitting next to someone hot on a plane is great, because they're a captive audience. Unlike at a bar, they can't say, "Be right back," and then disappear into a crowd. Though it's much more insulting when they try.

Trains

How is it that trains crash as often as they do? There are no tracks in the sky, and planes get along fine. One track, one train. Simple math.

I feel weird about walking into the dining car of a train if I'm not wearing a fedora.

You get various discounts on Amtrak if you have a Student Advantage card. So taking the train for several hours is now only a little more expensive than just flying there.

We have advanced so far technologically. We have all these conveniences like monorails and computerized automated announcements and e-tickets. But we can't seem to kick the habit of those funny little train hats.

If a grown man came over to you and said, "I enjoy playing with tiny replicas of methods of conveyance, while they speed past incredibly small plastic people with no faces and two fingers to each hand," you'd think he was crazy. But if someone said, "My dad's into model trains," then it's fine.

Every city calls their public train system something different. You've got the subway, the metro, the T, BART, SEPTA, MARTA, etc, etc, etc. Here's a thought: call it a train.

It would be fun if campuses had monorails. Not to ride on or anything. I would just enjoy saying, "Why the hell did they build a monorail?"

Automobiles

Parents get so excited about those little car stickers that say what school their kids go to. I don't mind them so much—it's a huge step forward from giving out a family newsletter.

It would be great, just once, to see one of those car window stickers with a note that says "Couldn't hack it— dropped out after three weeks."

College students would get a lot of use out of SUVs. Road trips would be easier to plan if we could just drive straight.

Last year, Florida State cancelled two days of classes to avoid congestion from a football game. A football game! I went to school in Manhattan—if we did this every time there was too much traffic, no one would have class from 6 to 10 in the morning, and again from 4 to 7 at night.

Some people drive to class when it's cold, which would make sense if you could find a parking spot. But if you walk half a block to your car, drive three blocks to class, and end up parking two blocks away, how much time outside did you really save?

People get really excited about road trips, because everyone likes going places. In a cramped car. For six hours.

Having a car helps expand your options of where to go for a night out. But being the one to drive it severely reduces your options once you get there.

Chapter 4

The Social Life

There are two kinds of parties in college: The Wild Party and The Get Together. At the first one, people complain when it ends by 4 AM, encourage visits from the police, and cheer for the next round of Natty Lite. At the second, it was supposed to be a Wild Party but not enough people showed so the host didn't want to admit that they under-promoted. Sure, there can be in-between parties, but either someone screams "Wooooo!" at the top of their lungs, or you sit on couches and talk about the midterm.

However you party, socializing in college is about spending time with people. A lot of time. Way too much time. You find some true friends along the way, but most of your colleagues are people that you see every day for years, and you somehow have to find new things to talk about right up until graduation. Luckily, our forefathers anticipated these problems. Right after the checks and balances system, Congress made parties really loud and schools large enough so that you can always meet new people with which to force conversation.

By my senior year, I had met enough people that I could go out by myself and chill with whomever I happened to meet up with along the way—sort of a friend Russian roulette. Inevitably, there were nights that I wanted to shoot myself in the head, but that is how the game works. But I should probably stay off the game analogy. That was the last chapter—and this is the social life.

Other Schools

Other schools are really just your school with different names on the buildings.

It took me four years to alienate all the girls I go to school with. But if I'm visiting another school, I can do it all in one weekend.

When you're deciding between schools, you look at every campus you visit and say, "Man, I could really fit in here." When you're visiting friends at the same school two years later, you say, "I'm sure glad I made the choice I did. I'd never fit in here."

I've visited a lot of campuses that have lakes. And every time I see one, whoever I'm with says, "Oh, yeah, that's the lake," like it's no big deal. We had a lake once. Then they called maintenance.

When you visit a friend, you say, "Don't worry, I'll just crash on the floor." Then it comes time for you to go to sleep, and you toss and turn till 5:00 AM, getting pissed at your friend for thinking you should sleep on the floor.

Some people prefer small schools because they like the individual attention and feeling of community. Except everyone in the community is apathetic about their school because it's so small that none of their other friends have heard of it.

Bragging about your school being in the news is OK, but only if it was in the news for the right reasons. "Hey, you know that toxic dumping that's been going on? That was us. Cool, huh?"

Friends

There are always people in your life you're friends with who aren't the coolest people you know. Which is fine until they ask you to set them up.

My friends get pissed off whenever I act like a jerk. So how do people who are jerks all the time make friends in the first place?

I think I have more attractive female friends than most guys have friends at all. And that's not saying I can attract cute girls—it's saying that I screwed up trying to get with them, and now I've got to settle for their friendship.

Friends are always there for you. Except when you have to move. Then they're there the next day.

Everybody knows one person who is totally nuts, and gets invited out just because you need a good story to tell the next day. And even though a million of these people are out there, for all of our safety, none of them are ever friends with each other. Because then every story in the entire world would start with, "And then he said, 'You think *that* was crazy?'"

I have been getting really tired of saying hi to casual acquaintances. But I still get really pissed if they don't say hi to me.

You need college friends after college for the sole purpose of being able to say, "Remember that time when…" and not having to end the sentence with "yesterday."

Greek Life

Being in a fraternity or sorority is just like being in a family. Except you decide who is born.

I love when someone really religious tells me that Greek life is weird. Yeah, sure. You think that your savior resides in a cracker, but a few guys with a handshake scare you.

No one who has ever worn a designer shirt can make fun of people who wear their Greek letters across their chest. When you wear Greek letters, you're representing something that you're very proud of. When you wear designer clothes, you're representing a guy named Abercrombie and another one named Fitch who bilked you into giving them $30 for a T-shirt you could have paid $2 for at a yard sale.

Some people asked me if they should join a fraternity so they could have things to put on their resume. No, that's why you get a job. You join a fraternity so you can have things to put on your calendar.

It must be surreal for Greek tourists to walk around in a college town, wondering what the hell we're trying to spell. All I'm saying is that if I were in Greece and saw "KFC," I'd expect chicken.

I wore my Greek letters in school a lot—especially during rush. But I will never understand the sororities that spent the week in those sweatpants with letters on their butts. During rush, your letters are an advertisement. And while the butt of a sorority girl is prime advertising space, you're marketing to the wrong audience.

Parties

When I throw a party, I want the girls to walk in thinking that they will absolutely, positively hate it there. Because girls hate parties for one main reason: too many girls.

Some colleges have a weird party scene, where parties keep getting shut down. So guests wander from house to house, looking for the next party that will get shut down in a half hour.

College parties and high school parties are very different. Because the wildest high school party you ever went to is only slightly better than a typical college Thursday night.

Throwing a good party is the easiest thing in the world. Just invite all the girls you know. You don't even have to tell any guys—they'll comb the neighborhood wondering where all the girls went until they end up at your place.

Live music at parties works if the music is good, but more important if the sound levels are okay. Nothing ruins a conversation like saying, "What? Could you, um, what? I can't…What?"

When you first join a fraternity, parties are incredible because there are all these new girls you don't know. I used to get so excited about our parties. But as I got older, I started to know everyone who came to them. And then the most fun part for me was watching the freshmen going, "Dude! Look at all of these girls we don't know!"

Smoking

I've contemplated taking up smoking. But I've also contemplated vacationing in the Caribbean, and I think that's cheaper.

The worst part about smoking is reeking of cigarettes, but that happens whenever you go out anyway. I think that's why some people smoke—if you are going to get jailed for assault, you may as well hit the guy.

Everyone looks awkward trying their first cigarette. And people who smoke always laugh, as if the same crap didn't happen to them.

It's hard to convince someone who's been smoking for years that cigarettes will kill them, since they're nowhere near death. That "truth" ad campaign would be much more effective if it showed kids things that affect them immediately. "In the winter, you're going to be outside in your pajamas smoking, and it's going to be really, really cold. The truth."

People who really like to eat love the smell of a bakery. People who really like to drive love the smell of gasoline. People who really like to play ball love the smell of freshly cut grass. But there are no people who walk by someone on their way home from a party, take a big whiff, and say, "Mmmm...stale bar smell."

When we were in high school, they tried bringing in a guy who spoke through a voice box in order to deter kids from smoking. And I swear half the class said, "You mean I could end up talking through a voice box? Awesome."

Bars

If you pay a cover and the bar sucks, leave. Do *not* stay and try to get your money's worth. Time is money. You've already spent the cover—don't let them keep charging you.

There should be a sign when you're leaving every bar that reminds you to drink a glass of water before you go to sleep.

Paying a cover to get $1 beers is okay if it's decent beer, but not if it's something like Natty Lite. Natty, Beast, PBR— that stuff is forty cents at the grocery store. And I know that you go to a bar for the ambience, but I'd hardly call Natty Lite ambience.

Bars that don't have a cabaret license won't let you dance. But they never have enough chairs, either.

It's all right for an older guy to be a regular at a college bar when there's nothing else in the area. But there were a dozen bars to choose from near my school, yet old guys went to the college bars anyway. The only thing worse than being sketchy is being voluntarily sketchy.

I used to wonder why they called it a bar. But it makes sense—after you leave, doesn't it feel like you got smacked upside the head with one?

Some professors divide your papers into three piles, alphabetically by last name, to avoid the crush of everyone trying to approach the desk at once. Why can't bars do that with last call?

Alcohol

I understand wanting a strong drink at a bar in order to get your money's worth. But if you're mixing at home, spread the liquor out a little. It tastes a lot better if you actually use mixers. But then you have to spend all that extra effort having three drinks instead of two.

Girls: beware of the guy who offers to buy you a Long Island iced tea. Guys: beware of the girl who asks for seconds.

Take your glasses off or your contacts out and look at yourself in the mirror—that's when you think you're at your most attractive. The same thing happens to your perception of other people when you drink. When the world gets a bit fuzzy, you fill in the blanks by hoping for the best.

My cousin was a traveling salesman, and used to go to bars and order a Bent Banana. The reason you've never heard of it is because he made it up just to prove that a bartender will never admit that he doesn't know how to make a drink. Usually, they'd give him something with banana liquor. But every once in a while, he'd get a guy who'd use an entire banana.

I used to want to have a drink named after me. But then I thought about people saying, "Oh man, I shouldn't have had that last Steve."

After you graduate, you can't drink as much. Sure, you have the same tolerance. But your willingness to wake up in your own puke has been tailing off since junior year.

The Definition of Drink
an observationalhumor.com classic

At a bar, often someone's first impression of you is what you're drinking. To help, here's a list of different drinks and what they'll mean to those around you.

Budweiser, Miller, or Coors

Guys: They don't have kegs at this bar? What kind of lowbrow place is this?

Guys buying it for girls: I don't celebrate anniversaries, I don't care about your friends, and as soon as you expect commitment, I will drop you. May as well get used to it.

Girls: Does drinking cheap beer make me look sexy and tomboyish?

Sam Adams, Honey Brown, or Pete's Wicked

Guys: I bet this beer tastes good because it costs more.

Guys buying it for girls: Work study? Hah! That's for suckers. I've got a swanky internship paying me $10 an hour!

Girls: Drinking cheap beer makes me look too tomboyish. Does drinking expensive beer make me look sexy?

Hard Lemondae, Smirnoff Ice, Cider, or Zima

Guys: That baguette was really filling.

Guys buying it for girls: I bet she doesn't know that this is just as alcoholic as beer.

Girls: Drinking any kind of beer makes me look too tomboyish. Good thing this is just as alcoholic.

Guinness

Guys: I don't intend to get drunk tonight. Thankfully, this beer takes a half hour to finish.

Guys buying it for girls: I don't want you to leave this bar for the next half hour.

Girls: I hope I'm not hung over during rugby tomorrow.

Natural Ice, Old Milwaukee, or Pabst Blue Ribbon

Guys: Hey, can I borrow a dollar?

Guys buying it for girls: If you think that's impressive, you should see the generic brand cereal we'll be eating tomorrow morning.

Girls: Man, that sex change was expensive.

Long Island Ice Tea

Guys: I'm not drunk enough yet to be charming. One of these should do it.

Guys buying it for girls: I don't think this girl is drunk enough yet to think I'm charming. One of these should do it.

Girls: I'm really easy, but I don't want to admit it. None of these guys is charming, but now I can blame it on the alcohol when I sleep with them.

Jack and Coke or Rum and Coke

Guys: I'm tired of beer, but I don't know anything about mixed drinks. Thank god this one is named after its ingredients.

Guys buying it for girls: I'm not playing around. I want you drunk and I want you drunk now.

THE SOCIAL LIFE

Girls: I haven't decided if I'm going to hook up with this guy or beat the crap out of him. I hope I'm not hung over during rugby tomorrow.

Midori Sour or Cosmopolitan

Guys: Hey, that bartender is kind of hot. I wonder what his name is?

Guys buying it for girls: I really like this girl. I can't wait for her to start picking out my clothes and telling me who I'm allowed to be friends with.

Girls: Why isn't anyone buying me any drinks? Maybe if I buy one for myself and act cute and girly, that guy over there will buy me one. Wait, he's talking to the bartender…

Whiskey Sour

Guys: I saw some guy order this in a movie once. I think he was a detective.

Guys buying it for girls: I saw some guy buy this for a girl in a movie once. I think he was a detective.

Girls: A girl has never ordered a whiskey sour.

Shot of Tequila

Guys: Hey, is someone stealing my tiny, very expensive red sports car?

Guys buying it for girls: I figure either we'll hook up or you'll pass out on my floor. Maybe a little of both.

Girls: Does anyone know where I put my birth control pills?

Sex on the Beach

Guys: That midori sour was a little weak.

Guys buying it for girls: See, it's got sex in the name. Get it? Like, it's just the name of a drink, but it says "sex". Understand?

Girls: Hey, the color of this drink matches my tube top!

Screwdriver

Guys: I can't believe that fake ID worked! Man, freshman year is gonna rock!

Guys buying it for girls: Is it cool if we make out in the corner for a while?

Girls: I wonder if this counts for my daily dose of vitamin C? Maybe I should get a Vodka Cranberry just in case.

Water

Guys: I better sober up so I don't pass out before I hook up with this girl.

Guys buying it for girls: I better get this girl sobered up so she doesn't pass out before we hook up.

Girls: I better sober up so I don't hook up with the guy who bought me all those drinks.

Chapter 5

Men and Women

Men and women are what make the world go round. Actually, that's centrifugal force. But there's a large amount of energy created by women slamming cabinet doors in disgust over what the men in their lives did. If every woman slammed a cabinet door at the same time, I bet the earth would spin the other way and time would rewind just like at the end of Superman I.

There are a few million theories on the differences between men and women, none more ridiculous than the idea that gender is an artificial construct of society. Last I heard, men and women look very different naked, no matter what society they're part of. And while there have been some very artificial things added to naked men and women, you get my point.

Women allege that men have it better because they have historically held higher paying jobs. But if men really did control things, don't you think they'd be the ones having multiple orgasms? If God were male, men would not be the ones falling asleep directly after sex. God is a woman, and she is smart enough to stop guys at one climax per session. Because if men had the ability to do that any more often, a man would be thirty-five before he left the house.

In college, sexual activity becomes a bit more prevalent than it used to be. We're older, we don't all live with our parents, and the condoms are free. God may not be a man, but any guy in college is thanking her. Right before he tries to hook up with her daughter.

Interaction

Face it: confidence is sexy, and indecisiveness is not. At least I'm pretty sure that's true. I think.

Men aren't trying to have sex with every woman they meet. Just the hot ones. I'm kidding, it's all of them.

A girl once asked me what pick-up line works on guys. I told her to go with, "Hello."

Every guy makes sexual innuendos sometimes, or talks about who he thinks is hot. And it's okay to let that stuff slip in front of a girl sometimes. But try not to let it be in front of the same girl every time. As soon as you do that more than twice, you go from being a guy who was being open and honest to being the biggest pervert this side of Ron Jeremy.

Why is there no good word to describe the stage between like and love? It's really embarrassing to say, "I loke you."

If you're with someone and you're not going to hook up, it's nice to know where you stand ahead of time. Because if the end of the night is known to be platonic, then you can have playful sexual tension. If only one person knows that it's platonic, then you can have playful sexual horribly awkward.

When I go anywhere with a lot of red tape—the post office, the DMV, financial aid—I always pray that the person behind the desk is an unattractive woman. Because if it's a guy, my flirting gets me nothing. And if it's an attractive woman, it gets me even less.

Differences

Women and men both think they're right about everything. Already, that's something about which men are wrong.

Most girls want to be Scarlett O'Hara. They want to be a strong woman who battles through and makes it, all while taming the crude Rhett Butler and making him fall for her. And that works perfectly, because most guys want to bang Scarlett O'Hara.

A lot of girls say that they won't have sex with a guy until they get to know him. A lot of guys say that about girls, too, but the girls actually mean it.

When a guy brings a girl to orgasm quickly, he takes it as a compliment. When a girl does it to a guy, she takes it as an insult.

If a guy is watching football in the forest, and no one is around to hear him, does he still yell at the TV?

Women buy clothes that specifically make their breasts look bigger. Guys do the same thing: buy clothes that make women's breasts look bigger.

Many girls like being treated like princesses. Many guys like showing off that they're dating girls who look like princesses.

Women are constantly looking for a guy when they are single with a bunch of attached friends. Men are constantly looking for a girl when they are breathing with a bunch of breathing friends.

Hooking Up

There are all these matching services that are trying to appeal to college kids, where they try to help students meet each other. There's a pretty good one I like—it's called "any friggin weekend."

Does it ruin the moment when you slide over so that you don't fall off the bed?

I wonder what girls are thinking about while they're hooking up. I usually think about nothing in particular, but that's normal for guys.

If you're a guy in college and you're still fumbling with bras, just go buy one and practice. It's a life skill just useful enough to study.

When a girl tries to be sexy by tying a cherry stem with her tongue, all I can think is, "Ow!"

Talent at hooking up will always be a surprise. Because that's something that no one will ever believe until you prove it to them. And it's not something you can talk about and then say, "I'm serious, wanna see?"

Every sexual harassment seminar tells you to ask permission before you do things. Which is okay, but do it *after* everyone else leaves the room.

A cute girl complaining to me about how she doesn't get enough play is like a venture capitalist complaining to me that he doesn't have anyone in which to invest his money. Unless I'm your solution, I don't want to help you figure out who is.

Dating

At some point, every couple needs to have a talk about what they are, no matter how risky it may be. It will help you avoid saying, "I think she's my girlfriend."

Relationships usually become exclusive ten minutes after the guy's friend starts hitting on the girl.

As romantic as an Italian restaurant can be on a date, be careful when you go there. Whatever you do, stay away from food you might have to slurp.

When a fraternity guy dates a sorority girl, their brothers and sisters get all excited. It's like being a nobleman while the King of France and the Queen of England start hooking up.

When a couple is asked if they're dating, they'd better keep quiet until they know if their answers match.

How can a college couple keep track of anniversaries? Does a first kiss only count if you were sober?

Moving to a new city after graduation helps you meet new people, but then you have no place to bring them on dates. "I know this one really nice restaurant. Oh, you want to go somewhere else? Because really, I only know this one restaurant."

Girls: when you say, "Honey, we need to talk," the suspense is awful. It's only fair that you give us an immediate idea of whether it's a good talk or a bad talk. A thumbs-up or thumbs-down would be very much appreciated.

Rejection

When someone says they just want to be friends, never say, "I have enough friends." Because if that quote gets around, you might not anymore.

The easiest time for a girl to realize that she doesn't like a guy is right after he buys her a really expensive dinner.

When you break up and can stay close with your ex's friends, it's a moral victory. Nothing heals a broken heart faster than saying, "Your friends like me better than you."

According to the law of averages, if you keep trying the same solution on various problems, your chances of solving one increase. Thus, if you keep asking people out, your chances of getting one date should increase. Except equations don't talk to each other. And potential dates do.

When you ask someone out, a lot of people think that the worst thing they can say is, "No." But having a laughing fit before they say, "No" is a little worse than just saying it.

The reason guys hit on girls they barely know is because rejection only stings when it's someone you care about. If you always hit on someone before you care about her, then you completely prevent that from happening.

It's all right to burn bridges. Just make sure you're on the right side first.

Chapter 6

Academics

The only thing that stopped me from taking caffeine pills to study was a poignant episode of "Saved by the Bell" where Jessie almost killed herself studying basic trig. Then I realized that she was supposed to be the smartest girl in high school, and yet she was already a junior and couldn't grasp the difference between sine and cosine. How does she expect to get into the Harvard of the west coast? I mean, come on!

By the time I got through with that thought process, I'd already stayed up through the night without the help of any artificial stimulants. Except the thought of Kelly in a bikini. Raaaaar.

Everyone finds their own way to study, and I never use anything to help me stay awake. Mainly because I am a flipping idiot if I don't get enough sleep the night before an exam. Knowing this as a weakness, I study as if the exam is eight hours before it actually takes place, so I will always get enough rest. College is all about playing to your strengths and combating your weaknesses. This only works, however, when your weakness is not an inability to identify weaknesses.

It's funny that College Jeopardy is easier than regular Jeopardy, because college is when you know a lot more random facts. I already know less than I did at graduation, mainly because no one has tested me on anything since. If they did, I guess I'd be kind of excited. So excited. So excited. Yet simultaneously so…scared. And if you didn't get that reference, you might be too entrenched in your academics.

Registration

I find it ironic when too many people try to register for a basic economics class.

I can understand when the advance copies of the course guides have some wrong information, because things change. But when you're trying to register for a course that has no date, time, or professor, you could use a little guidance.

I think students would work harder if schools let us register for our courses in order of GPA.

Columbia finally implemented computer registration, which is awesome. I hear next year, they're going to let us pay our tuition using these new "credit card" things I've been hearing so much about.

Everyone is always trying to find the best classes to take. "Have you taken any good classes? What classes should I take? Is this a good class?" Sure, it's a good class—for a writer interested in American History. You, on the other hand, are pre-law and kind of enjoy physics. So choose your own damn class and stop asking me what I like.

A lot of schools have "pre-registration" the semester before classes start. But "pre-registration" is an abstract term. I prefer "false sense of security."

When you get to school, you're going to want to take a few classes that will change your life. By the time you graduate, you'll want to take a few lives that have changed your classes.

Books

When you are given a book for class, you don't want to read it. It doesn't matter if it's the best book of all time; you will not want read it. If it were sitting on your friend's desk, you might pick it up and stay up all night with it. But because you have a week to get through the thing, you won't get past the third chapter.

Why do all of your professors ignore the titles and instead refer to your textbooks by the last name of the author?

So often, professors assign books that are full of theories long since proven wrong. I once asked why. Frankly, "I had to read it when I was your age" is not an acceptable answer.

For someone who makes his living off people who read books, I make an awful lot of jokes about how I don't read other people's.

Why do professors get more upset if you show up for class having not done the reading than if you skipped class entirely?

Some people skip the reading and instead use the Cliffs Notes to save time. And to these people, I say, "Cliffs Notes are eighty pages! I don't have time for eighty pages!"

When you actually do the reading, you feel so smart, like you understand things better than anyone in the class. And then you realize, "Oh wait—this is how the rest of them always feel."

Studying

Right before I take an exam, I know every last thing about everything I studied. And a day later, I remember it all. And a few weeks later, I'll have taken another exam, so I'll know everything for that one. And nothing from that first test.

There are all these study skills workshops available to college students. But I'm going to save you a lot of time and just summarize them for you: try not to forget crap.

I'm a history major because I can only really remember stuff in story form. Sure, you get that in other subjects too, but stories about mitosis aren't so enthralling.

I had a friend who used to sit in Spanish Harlem when she wanted to study Spanish because it would help her to be immersed in it. I wonder if she ever interrupted anyone and asked them to talk about the contents of a kitchen or what Jose's father does at work.

I'm waiting for the day that they come out with pre-highlighted textbooks.

When I'm done studying, and I think I know a subject really well, I go over it one more time with a friend of mine from class. Not to be certain that I know what I'm talking about—I just want to be sure that they know less than I do.

You get pretty conditioned in school. I was so used to studying history that the first time I did a stand-up routine, I made flash cards.

Classes

Giving your class 200 pages of reading on the first day is like throwing someone off a cliff to see if they can fly. When someone actually completes that amount of reading that early, I'm always tempted to yell, "She's a witch! Burn her!"

I understand when high schools can't afford to fund certain popular classes because they can't get anyone to teach them. But private universities always have the money; they'd just rather spend it on really nice office furniture.

If customer service calls can be recorded for training purposes, why can't classes?

I've certainly taken some great classes—even a few that I enjoyed going to. But I have never taken a class to which I've actively looked forward. Deciding *not* to hit the snooze button on my alarm is about all the enthusiasm I can muster.

When you take a 300-level course instead of a 100-level course, why don't you learn three times as much?

Why are life skills classes looked down upon? If you have electives, spend them on stuff you're going to actually use. Take an extra physics class? No! Learn what to do when you forget to pay your electric bill? Sure!

I don't know which classes I have to go to by which day of the week it is. I know which day of the week it is by which classes I have to go to.

Midterms

There are thousands of colleges out there, each with a different schedule for midterms. And each with at least one professor who doesn't care about the schedule, and gives a midterm two weeks after you thought you were done.

I think it's disgusting that they make us study for midterms during Columbus Day. Don't they know how solemn that day is? Especially when the Monday on which it happens to be celebrated coincides with the actual day?

When you stay in and study for midterms during the spring semester, you have spring break to look forward to. When you stay in and study for midterms during the fall semester, you have crappy cold weather to look forward to.

A midterm is like a final's bratty little brother. Sure, the monstrous final can punch you in the gut, knocking the wind out of you. But the midterm could still poke you to death.

When there are recognizable names for sickness or pain, people accept it better. You may have flu-like symptoms, so you tell people that you have the flu so that you don't have to explain why your symptoms, though not really the flu, are just as bad. This is the same logic that makes people refer to September exams as midterms.

I don't think playing solitaire helps me study for a midterm, but I sure do enjoy it.

Papers

I like writing papers much more than taking exams. You can finish a paper a week early if you need to for your schedule. You can study for an exam a week earlier, but only if you're willing to forget everything and study again.

I am proud to have completed seventeen years of school never once having prepared a bibliography or footnotes the exact right way.

How much does it suck to use an online source for a paper and then find out that the page is down when it's time to turn in the damn thing?

My first draft of my paper is usually my final draft with a few typos. But some people actually have actual drafts, where the first one is made up of incoherent thoughts and incomplete sentences. If you have the ability to write well by the time you hand in the sucker, why not just start out that way?

If you plan to use Courier New on your final paper, you better start using it on everything you turn in. Because if you were worried that a professor might figure out that your font is bigger than everyone else's, you may want to make sure that it's not also bigger than your own.

If anyone complains that their thesis is boring, that's their fault. Long? Sure. Tedious? Of course. Time consuming? Definitely. But you picked your thesis. If you couldn't come up with one thing that wasn't boring, it's not your paper that sucks.

Finals

I could never take a class pass/fail. If I aced the final, I'd be mad at myself for doing well.

You can't understand finals unless you have them. A semester after you've graduated, your friends with finals disappear on you, and you can't figure out why. You know that rough project you have at work? Make it three times as hard. Now do five of them in the next week, and see how often you can meet for drinks.

Isn't the idea of having more than one final a little contradictory?

When finals are over, they're over, and that is what matters. You can't go back and change your answers, so it's best to just move on. Especially if you have to retake the class the following semester.

If everyone in America worked as hard all the time as most students do during finals week, we'd have had flying cars before the Civil War.

When you get out of a final, people always ask you how you did. But all I know after a final is what I thought the right answers were. It matters a lot more what the professor thought the right answers were.

The worst thing about finals is that you can't argue for partial credit. How many times have teachers added wrong on other exams, or have you managed to argue your way to a few extra points? That's a lot harder to do when you're not given the test back until after you've forgotten the professor's name.

I Know This Kid Who Did This Thing
a myth about college myths

Tell you a little bit about myself? Sure.

Someone once asked me what courage was, and I said, "This." I've been known to knock a pile of papers off my professor's desk and shove mine in the middle because he didn't know my name. And I routinely copy off the kid next to me, and forget to use my name instead of his.

After arriving late to a final because of a flat tire, my buddies and I were given a one-question exam asking us which tire. I mistook the infinity symbol for a sideways eight, and thus answer other questions with sideways numbers. I drew a mathematical proof for hell being endothermic based on a girl turning me down in high school.

I once woke up in a bathtub with my kidneys missing, but it was my fault for drinking the unlabeled punch. I'm glad I didn't turn the light on because if I had, the guy who hacked up my roommate would have gotten me, too. And I've learned that it's quite easy to mistake a guy licking your hand for the familiar slobber of your family dog.

I avoid cars with no headlights at all costs. I frequent Internet chat rooms, but I use my real name to avoid accidentally having sex with a family member. And I hand in essays like these.

But I have not yet been to college.

Chapter 7

The Supporting Cast

College, like the world in which it exists, is full of millions of different people, each bringing with them their unique stories of loss, redemption, love, and heartache. For the purposes of this chapter, those millions of people will become, say, a dozen.

OK, there are more than twelve different types of people in college. But most of them repeat. The rooms may change. The names may vary. The hometowns may differ. But so many people are caricatures of themselves that senior pictures should all have giant faces and rollerskates.

Every a capella group has at least one member who sings with a liiiiiittle too much passion. Every writing class has the guy who can't grasp grammar, on whom the teacher inexplicably goes easy. Every sorority has a girl whose bid, though unanimous, remains a mystery to everyone. That's why RAs make signs for people's doors. Without them, you wouldn't be able to tell most people apart. Think about it—

what do those signs usually say? A room number. A name. And sometimes a hometown. Because that is all that really differentiates us.

Hey you: the guy who can't get through bio class without three cell calls, make sure your ringer is on. Pink shirt girl: you need to be at your desk ignoring all the guys ogling your pink shirt. And Mr. Guard: is that a big enough chip on your shoulder? Who works in wardrobe anyway? Places everybody! The scene is about to begin.

High School Friends

After college, you get this tremendous desire to catch up with your high school friends. Then you remember why you haven't talked to them in four years.

Remember in high school how you used to sit next to that really attractive girl in your freshman English class? She doesn't.

There will always be jocks and there will always be cheerleaders, no matter how old you get. They just won't be wearing the uniforms.

Some people I went to high school with have done really interesting things. One was on the Real World, another won The Amazing Race, and one was in porn. Why do I get the feeling that last girl is the only one who got a harsh dose of reality?

Some students seek out people from their high school who wound up going to the same college. Why do this? You know how varied your high school was? You know how many people you didn't get along with? Assuming you can be friends with someone just because they went to the same high school is like assuming that everyone with your first name likes the same crap you do.

In the four years you're on campus, you run into three people from your high school and it's only because they went to the same college. Within a month after graduation, you'll have run into one in a department store, two in an airport, and seventeen who happened to move to whatever city you did.

Parents

Why do parents get upset when their kids go away to college? I think it'd be the biggest relief in the world. You know how nice it is when your roommate goes away for a long weekend and you get the place all to yourself? Same principle.

Parents ask their kids the weirdest questions. My mom once asked me if I had enough shoes. Shoes? Shoes are not something you run out of. When you do, you really have no choice but to buy more. And what made her think of asking me? "You know, there's been more sharp stuff on the ground lately. I wonder if Steve has been wearing enough shoes."

You get along much better with your parents after you go away to school. For the same reason it's a lot easier to be friends with your former boss once you're working at another company.

When you commute to school and live with your folks, you trade freedom for certain conveniences. Like laundry, food, and celibacy.

It's cool when your parents want to be more open with you as you're becoming an adult, but it is never cool for them to make sexual references to each other. How horrible is that to picture? Okay, so maybe you weren't picturing it. But you are now.

The longer you live away from home, the more likely you'll get along with your parents. It's not because you're maturing; they realize that unless they ease up, you'll exercise your option of not coming back.

Siblings

My older brother got mad at me for not visiting him enough while I was at school. Sure, he lived in a nice house with a wife and two kids. But I lived in a place with a bunch of my friends, where everyone partied on the weekend, hung out on weekdays, and rarely went to sleep before 2:00 AM. And he wanted *me* to come visit *him*?

How come bars always let in the 15-year-old little brother but never the 19-year-old friend?

If you don't want your friends to hit on your sister, stop introducing her to all of them.

I couldn't imagine going to the same school as one of my siblings. I changed a *lot* between high school and college. The last thing I needed was someone standing behind me going "He's nothing like this. He's really a much bigger dork than you think."

Did you apply to colleges that your older siblings got rejected from just to see if you could get in? Because, uh, a friend of mine did that. Yeah, a friend of mine.

Living with siblings beforehand makes college so much easier. Because when you're living with a roommate you can't stand, all you have to do is compare one year to fifteen years, and it's a lot easier to stomach.

The day you go away to college you will feel more free than you've ever felt up to that point in your life. It narrowly edges out how free you felt the day that your older sibling went away to college a few years back.

Students

When you like someone at school, you remember them even after graduation. You may have met them once, didn't even have a conversation, and yet you know everything about them. You need to be careful when this happens, because after graduation people will constantly play the name game with you. "Oh, did you know someone named Jim Smith?" "Uh, no. His class schedule and eating habits sound familiar, but I can't put a finger on why."

People get all defensive when I'm not interested in their major. "Oh, so bio-med isn't good enough for you?" Relax buddy, it's good enough. It's just not *easy* enough.

Some students are natural leaders. But some just happen to hold leadership positions. You can tell the difference by watching what happens when food arrives late to an event. Natural leaders will calm the crowd and order more food. People who just happen to hold leadership positions will pace back and forth before frantically asking why everything bad happens to them.

Why do philosophy students quote their readings at bars? You don't see math students scribbling integers on bar napkins. And if you do, leave the bar.

Students look for a sense of pride in whatever their school is good at, no matter how little it has to do with them. This is most commonly done by bragging about sports teams, the size of an endowment, or the world-renowned biology department when you're a communications major.

Roommates

You're incredibly lucky if you become friends with as many as five percent of all the people you meet. In freshman dorms, there are usually about twenty people on your floor. So the odds that the one you live with is also the one that you can stand are very, very slim.

If you have a choice your freshman year, for the love of all that is holy, choose a single. Taking on a roommate you don't know is like sitting next to a stranger on a transatlantic flight. For the next 250 days.

Your first roommate will either have nothing to contribute to the room or will bring the same exact stuff you do.

How embarrassing is it when your roommate has really bad taste in posters? "Dude, that's not my side of the room. No, I'm not a Hanson fan."

Two roommates dating two roommates is the perfect cosmic balance. There may be four people and two rooms, but everyone will always have a single.

Some people are really easy to live with. Some people are hell to live with, but they have really big TVs so it's OK.

When you're roomed with a complete loser—and I'm talking about the kind of loser that even recognizes how big of a loser he is—it can be seen as an unfortunate coincidence.

Or it can be seen as someone in the school administration thinking that you two would really get along.

Professors

It's weird to call a professor by his first name. When someone can determine my entire future based on a pen stroke, I can't just call him Bob.

If I were a hot professor, I would totally mess with people's heads. Students are already supposed to believe what professors tell them, and anyone would believe anything an attractive member of the opposite sex said. Add the two together and that's power. If I were a hot professor, every last one of my students would leave class thinking that the capital of North Dakota is seven.

Nothing makes an incredibly difficult class worthwhile like a truly dynamic professor. And nothing makes it worthless like a truly dynamic professor sitting in the back of the room while a TA botches the lesson plan.

A lot of professors don't enjoy office hours. That's why they tell you about them on the first day of class. Even they know that no one is writing anything down yet.

The root of the word "professor" is "profess." But when was the last time you heard that word associated with anything other than love? "And thus, the Monroe Doctrine has dictated how we handle foreign policy. Honeylips."

The professor on *Gilligan's Island* was a dead-on portrayal. How many of your professors, while being the only semi-attractive guy on an island with two gorgeous women, would spend all their time on crappy experiments? All of them.

Administrators

There were some administrators at my school who never did anything other than schmooze with potential trustees. I know that these administrators weren't always like that—there's got to be a point where their career paths changed. "You've done a wonderful job with academic initiatives and housing directives, but my question is, can you cut ribbons?"

If none of the top-ten ranked people at a college attend a school sporting event, why should the rest of us?

Our tuitions are not high because we pay for new buildings or top-tier professors. They're high because schools have a 4:1 dean:student ratio.

There are hundreds of administrators at your school, and every last one of them is too busy to talk to you.

School administrators are in a no-win situation. Either they rarely talk to their students, which makes them standoffish, or they spend plenty of time with their students, which makes them arrested.

Some students are best friends with administrators. They're always in the office of some dean or another, talking about what they did that weekend or who they tried to get with. I'm not supporting age discrimination, but you live with thousands of people your own age. Can't you be friends with at least one of them?

I have a theory that deans really don't do much during the day, but their secretaries turn away kids for the effect. It's like waiting in line for a bar that's half empty.

Alumni

When you come back to visit school after you graduate, don't be surprised when things look different. While I was an undergrad, my school tore down two buildings, built three, and renovated at least four dorms. So when I came back and I didn't recognize the guard at the main entrance, it wasn't a big deal.

Wanting to visit your freshman room after you graduate is kind of pointless, since the rooms all look the same. "This is where I used to keep my stereo. Or was it my computer? Maybe it was my mini fridge. Crap, is this even my room?"

If you were a big shot on campus, try not to visit until several years after you graduated. Otherwise, you'll puzzle at why the current big shots are people you remember as puny freshmen. And you'll completely forget that you once were, too.

If schools were smart, they'd wait until you paid off your student loans before asking you for a donation.

When you wear an alumni shirt from your school, people will always ask you if you went there. So you say "Sure," and the logical question to then ask them is what year they went. And they inevitably say, "Oh, I never went to college. But some kid I knew from high school almost went there. Small world, huh?"

When I went back to visit my high school a year after graduation, all the freshmen looked really tiny. When I went back to visit my college a year after graduation, all the freshmen looked really hot.

Bouncers

When bouncers throw a party, who works the door?

During the summer, bouncers have to wear tight black T-shirts. I don't know if it's a local law or a federal law, but I know it's a law.

I've never seen a bouncer successfully bounce a person on the sidewalk. But I've seen lots of them try.

A bouncer is a limited profession—you don't see many of them older than forty. So bouncers—while you don't have to treat any of the bar-goers nicely while you're working, you might want to try it anyway. Your resume is probably limited already; the last thing you need is someone from HR recognizing you as the prick that wouldn't let him in two days before his 21st birthday.

Bouncing work doesn't pay all that well, but it makes you an instant celebrity. What other job makes the entire world kiss up to you, yet pays only $10 an hour?

Bouncers should sell phony IDs. They have access to the market, they know what makes a good fake, and at any time, they are the only ones who can guarantee it will work.

Dear Mr. Bouncer,

Please excuse Steve from being carded tonight. His ID has been feeling ill lately.

Thank you,
Mrs. Steve's Mom

Guards

Guards are RAs who don't get free housing.

A campus security guard is a profession that few people choose—it's something that people fall into. So he may be on campus, and he may be guarding something, but some guy who is only there because he has to be isn't my idea of security.

Has a guard ever checked what you wrote when you signed in a guest? I once signed in my friend using the guard's name, just to see if he would notice.

Guards get paid to sit and check IDs all day. They're like bouncers with chairs.

I don't think all security guards are sports fans, but all other AM radio stations are boring.

Working security at a bank can get pretty scary, because people might try to rob the place. Working security at a college is even scarier because people might try to have sex in the stacks.

When there was all that rioting on college campuses in the late 1960s, what was going through the guards' minds? They had to have been thinking, "Oh man, I should have taken that cushy job at the all-night liquor store."

Sometimes guards stop people from making out on campus because it's against campus regulations. I do not support PDA and never will, but I would love to see that page in the rulebook.

Janitors

My senior year, we had this really cool janitor. He wasn't that much older than us and was someone we totally would have hung out with if we'd met under different circumstances. Instead, he scrubbed our toilets.

If you live in a janitor building, you don't get prepared for the real world. It's a rude awakening to find out that instant spray-and-wipe cleaning stuff is just a myth.

It'd be pretty easy to be a janitor in a college dorm. Sure, there's mess everywhere. But if you ever don't feel like cleaning something, you can just leave it for a day and pretend it's new mess.

Does it matter what colleges you work at when you are a janitor? Are future employers more impressed that you cleaned up Harvard puke?

We were told to call our janitors "porters" because that's the new name for the job. Like that changes anything? The same thing happened about ten years ago when secretaries became administrative assistants. Well, it's ten years later and we all know that an administrative assistant still takes notes and still gets coffee. So how long will it be before everyone knows that a porter cleans toilets?

The most hated phrase in a college janitor's vocabulary is "foam party."

It's probably worse being an indoor janitor than being an outdoor janitor. Sure, there's a lot more vomit outside, but you can't hose down a hallway.

Resident Advisors

When you go in for your RA interview, it's not a good idea to say, "And I can keep all the booze I confiscate, right?"

At every school I've visited, the RA comes up with a theme for writing people's names on doors. I've seen fruits, animals, furniture, cities, landmarks, cartoon characters, wonders of the world—everything. But just once, I want to see an RA who has the balls to write their residents' names on cardboard cutouts of beer bottles and cigarette packs.

No matter how good their sense of humor might be, I've found that very few RAs appreciate it when you yell, "Narc!"

I love when RAs threaten the administration with organizing their students in order to get something done. You couldn't even get a study break done. And there, you had the allure of free pizza.

When you're an RA, you do have some responsibility. But you are not a god. You are not even a security guard.

My friend had an RA who was a Libertarian, which I thought was one of the funniest things I'd ever heard. Think about it for a minute: that party's central platform is that a government should not interfere to protect their citizens from harming themselves. And regardless of my personal political stance on that issue, the people who believe in it shouldn't be pouring out someone else's booze.

Chapter 8

Facilities

No matter what the facilities are like on your campus, you will complain about them. At some schools, you have student centers with a food court bigger than your local mall. At some schools, you have gyms with the most expensive equipment you'll ever use. At some schools, you have libraries with more in-depth catalogues than Congress. Yet we still complain. Why? Because it can always be better.

"I visited my friend's school and his food court has *two* Taco Bells."

"I visited my friend's school and her gym has television sets by the bikes, and they all play *Sex and the City.*"

"I visited my friend's school and his library has the complete works of Shakespeare. The originals. Signed."

In actuality, when you visit your friend's school you see their lobby, room, bathroom, and wherever that one party was. But that doesn't stop you from taking these wild claims back with you. And what makes them believable are the obvious deficiencies you can point out in the facilities on your own campus.

My new student center is pretty incredible. But it's also awful at the same time. Despite all its conveniences and technological wizardry, half the thing is taken up by ramps. In the middle of Manhattan. Did I mention Columbia is cramped for space? Of course I'm going to complain! Besides, I visited my friend's school...

Dorms

I went my whole college career without locking my key in my room. So the summer after graduation, I lived in the dorms during an internship program. And the last week I was there, I left my key in my room. And you know where my roommate happened to be that one time? Neither do I.

Study lounge is a crappy name for a place where everyone studies but no one lounges.

NYU dorms are ridiculously expensive—I'm talking around $11,000 a year. Now, it's true that you can't get a studio in downtown Manhattan for less than $900 a month, which comes out to just under $11,000 for a year. But when you pay for a studio, you get a kitchen, more than eighty square feet, and the ability to light candles and turn on halogen lamps whenever the hell you want. When you pay for a dorm room, you get an RA.

In college, futons are everywhere. College students like to be able to sit down and pass out in the same place.

Choosing housing numbers would be so much more fun if they let you spin for it like on *Wheel of Fortune*.

When you graduate from college, you don't own any furniture. And it's not because you couldn't afford it—it's because you had no place to keep it.

You know why they don't convert dorms into hotels for the summer? Because no one with a choice would pay to stay in a dorm.

Bathrooms

When they came up with the idea for bathroom stalls, did they know people would lock them from the inside and crawl out underneath, laughing hysterically?

I will never take more than fifteen minutes in the bathroom in the morning. But I also have really short hair. The last time I tried to comb it, it laughed at me.

College bathrooms do get cleaned, so they're not always nasty. But you never know when they become nasty, so you're still just as terrified. The place could be sparkling, but until you know for sure what is behind that door, it's tough to go in there with confidence.

Men's college bathrooms are almost always white, yellow, or a combination of the two. More often than not, though, they started just white.

After graduation, I shared one bathroom with four other guys, and we never had a problem. In college, I shared four bathrooms with ten guys, and they were all always full.

One of these days, they're going to come up with a lock for a bathroom stall that you can't jimmy open with a nickel.

Sometimes you go into the bathroom and there's shampoo all over the top of the sink. I mean everywhere, like the bottle exploded. And instead of thinking, "What the hell could have made a bottle of shampoo explode?" we have been conditioned to think, "Again?"

Dining Halls

I don't think it's fair that dining halls are allowed to name a food something that it clearly is not.

I love the college dining halls with the gigantic tables; thirty-five people could fit on one side of them. Every time I see a table like that, I think, "Man, if they ever decide to move the dining hall, there's no way they're getting that thing out the door."

Right before they close, the dining hall should be willing to take five bucks for all their extra pasta.

One year, my class tried to donate all of our unused meal plan meals to the homeless. But the school wouldn't let us, saying that those unused meals were already factored into the cost of preparation. So thousands of students are being charged more per meal than it costs to eat in most Italian restaurants, yet the fifty extra meals we each have at the end of the semester have already been factored in? We couldn't have possibly taken *that* much silverware.

As colleges go, mine had pretty decent food in the dining hall. As the rest of civilization goes, I'd hesitate to call it food.

You know how they say that even bad pizza is good pizza? That's only true when you can tell that it's pizza.

Have you ever tried to get into the dining hall as it's supposed to close? They have vats of leftover food, but if you get there at 8:01, they'd rather throw it away than sell it to you.

Libraries

I used to be terrified of going into the stacks. Then I figured out how to work the lights.

At some school libraries, you can renew your books without even bothering to bring them back. Which is very convenient for everyone except the people waiting to borrow them.

If you don't have a reserve desk in your library, they work like this: the professor leaves the desk with one copy of the reading, which is available to borrow for short periods of time. During that time, you can either read a few pages or make copies of it for more than it would have cost to just buy the book. But the one plus this system has is giving people a way to *say* they did the reading when they never bothered to buy the book.

All it takes to get into your campus library is your school ID, but most of our libraries don't allow guests. Because only cretins from other schools would steal from your library, right?

We've already got Citibank, Taco Bell, and Pepsi all over my campus. I give it two years before they turn the library copy room into a Kinkos.

There are some books that are constantly being checked out. But there are others that haven't been looked at in decades. A friend of mine was a legacy at school, and told his father about a paper he was writing. His father recommended a few books that he'd used for a similar paper—and it turned out that no one had checked them out since.

The Gym

We have access to the best gyms most of us will ever see, yet we barely use them. And it's simply because we're not paying. If we had to give the gym even five bucks a year to use it, we'd be there lifting, squatting and pressing every last penny's worth.

The gym helps you only if you actually work out while you're there.

The problem with going to the gym for the first time in a while is you try to work out as much as you did the last time you were there. If you haven't run in the last year, don't try to start out with ten laps around the track. If you haven't benched since high school, don't try to beat your personal best. If you haven't done a pull up since you were twelve, you're not going to be able to do more than five. The human body doesn't work like that. Actually, after you do any of that to it, the human body doesn't work at all.

Getting buff at the gym helps guys attract girls. Getting sore at the gym doesn't. Nothing's sexier than a guy who can't lift his own arms.

The gym being near your dorm is convenient, but it being far away is better. You may go less often, but when you do, you'll work harder to avoid an extra trip.

People who regularly go to the gym don't talk about it much—you could be friends with someone for years before finding out that they work out four times a week. But someone who uses the gym once in a while lets everybody know every single time. Twice.

Chapter 9

Holidays and Events

There seem to be fewer and fewer holidays as you get older. Growing up, I remember those administrative half-days, when randomly throughout the year, we would get out early from school. I don't know if they did this everywhere, but it was wonderful. And it doesn't happen anymore. Mainly because college *is* a half-day.

College, aside from being waaaaaaay more fun than high school, is on a much better schedule. You have to start a week earlier, but you get out a month earlier. In high school, you had five days a week of about eight hours a day; in college you typically have four days a week of about four hours a day. And did I mention the month off in the middle to regroup? College is a giant holiday. And that's not enough for some people.

"Why do my classes start before eleven?"

"Why don't finals just start in April?"

"How come we don't get President's Day off anymore?"
Because we get President's Month off instead.

But somehow, we still need to find ways to unwind. We find holidays that give us three-day weekends even though some of our *schedules* give us three-day weekends. To find new rituals that break up the monotony of our daily lives, so we instead have monotony with tinsel. And to find just one more excuse for being self-celebratory—aside from, "Hey, I'm in college."

Birthdays

People get so incredibly selfish on birthdays. "We have an exam? But it's my birthday!" "What do you mean you're not coming out to party? It's my birthday!" "We just invaded Poland? But it's my birthday!" It's nice that you want to celebrate your birthday and all, but you really had nothing to do with it. If anything, we should be buying drinks for your parents.

People are still surprised when they meet other people who share their birthday. There are only 366 possible birthdays out there—how few people have you met that this "coincidence" still surprises you?

Some people like going to a random bar on their twenty-first birthday so that they can get carded. I think it's more fun to go to the one you've been going to for years, where you've never had to show ID. And then do it anyway. It's fun to say, "Look, I'm twenty-one," to someone who thought you were already twenty-five.

After you turn twenty-one, your plans get screwed up when you forget that many of your friends are younger. Especially if you're dating a freshman.

Birthday cakes have gone a bit out of style now that we've gotten older. Because now we have to pay for them.

Some people talk about their birthday a full month before it happens. Maybe they're excited about actually making it through another year because we almost killed them the last time they wouldn't shut up about their birthday.

Halloween

If you want to give a good scare, carve your pumpkin a few weeks early, and leave it outside to rot. Nothing frightens people quite as well as a rotted Jack O'Lantern with flies shooting out of its mouth.

Some people wear a lot of black to celebrate Halloween. I do it to celebrate New York.

Every year, my fraternity house makes sure we have candy to give to neighborhood kids in case they come by. Sure, we are there to help, but I can't imagine everyone at our school is. Whenever I handed a kid a piece of candy, I wanted to give their parents a note with it that said, "Stop bringing your kids trick-or-treating at a damn college!"

Some people start decorating for Halloween as soon as October comes around. If I were Columbus, I'd feel a bit slighted.

November first is one of the best shopping days of the year. Go into any drug store, drop ten bucks on the counter, and they'll give you so much candy you'll need to drive home.

Wouldn't it be fun to go up and down the dorm hall trick-or-treating for beer and condoms?

Some Halloween costumes are really creative. But no matter how brilliant your costume is, it's nothing if it's not recognizable. There are few things sadder than a guy wearing a carburetor and a packet of Earl Grey and swearing that he's the industrial revolution.

Election Day

I feel a kinship toward politicians. As a writer, it's also my job to steal from the world around me.

Some of the negative campaign ads are done wrong if they're targeting college students. "Jennifer Davidson missed almost a dozen votes while she was in Congress, yet she swears she was at all of them. Can the public trust someone who lies about their attendance?" I hope so, because, um, we do too.

Voting the year after a presidential election is like going to an optional discussion session. Yes, it helps to be there. But if you're unable to get there, you don't even bother to call someone the next day to see what you missed.

There was one year that I didn't make it to the polls in time. Thankfully, my candidates lost by more than one vote.

Our schools always make a big deal about apathy when only half of us vote in a student council election. But they don't seem to care that those numbers are a lot better than the rest of the country come November.

There are a lot of things to learn about voting when you first start. You have to remember to register, know what precinct to go to, change your address at least two months before an election if you move, and I still don't know when (or if it's ever better) to use an absentee ballot. There are a billion ads telling us to exercise our constitutional right. Is it so much to ask for just one telling us how?

Thanksgiving

A few hundred years ago, a turkey and a bunny were sitting there, and the turkey was laughing hysterically. "You mean they have a holiday where they dress you up in silly hats?," said the turkey. "Man, that's got to be the worst thing ever." And then came the Pilgrims.

An RA asked me if I could help her draw a turkey for Thanksgiving. I instinctively started tracing my hand.

The best part about Thanksgiving is not the time off from classes, it's not the huge meal, and it's not the TBS movie marathons. It's being able to read the label imprint on the cranberry sauce after it's out of the can.

I looked forward to Thanksgiving much more when I was in high school. You know, when I had Friday classes.

You know you're getting old when you watch the Thanksgiving Day Parade and don't recognize some of the balloons. You know you've already gotten old when you watch the Thanksgiving Day Parade and *do* recognize some of the singers.

When you go home for Thanksgiving, that's usually the best you'll eat all semester. I'm always tempted to tell my mom I'm bringing friends so we have more leftovers.

Thanksgiving is pretty ironic for college students. We come home to a gaggle of cheek-pinchers, we can't see any of our friends from school, and it's all with finals and papers hanging over us. This is what we're given? Thanks.

Christmas & Hannukah

There are several dozen accepted ways of spelling "Hannukah." None of them involve a Q.

Most dorms don't let you have candles in your room unless they're Hannukah candles. The cool thing is that no one knows when the hell Hannukah is, so between October and January, you can have all the candles you want.

I feel guilty accepting Christmas presents. Not because I don't celebrate the thing, but because I'm too cheap to buy them for anyone else.

Dorms try to be politically correct and have electric menorahs in the lobby in addition to the Christmas trees, yet they can't seem to ever light the right number of fake candles. "We light two on the first day? Does that mean we light four on the second day?" You light two on the first, three on the second, four on the third ...it is not a hard pattern to decipher. You expect us to remember that the RA schedule flips every third Monday and fourth Tuesday, but you can't seem to grasp the idea of "add one."

It's not hard to be a Jew on Christmas. But to be a Jew on Christmas doing anything other than watching a movie or eating Chinese food? That's next to impossible.

The reason Jewish kids are always looking to date other Jewish kids has nothing to do with having Jewish children. It's so that there will be less of a chance of their menorah setting a tree on fire.

New Year's

My New Year's resolution is going to be learning what the heck "Auld Lang Syne" means.

If you think of a resolution to better yourself at the beginning of December, you should start it that moment instead of waiting until New Year's. After all, it will only last a week anyway.

If I were Catholic, I'd give up making New Year's resolutions for lent.

As college students, our years are based around the academic calendar, not the Gregorian calendar. But we still celebrate New Year's with everyone else. Face it—no one wants to lead the countdown to the first day of classes.

Some people try to have someone to kiss every New Year's. Some people try to have someone to kiss every weekend.

A lot of bars have those countdown clocks that they reset for different events, and people are always asking what the next event is. The answer ranges: Thanksgiving, the Super Bowl, graduation. But when it's December 2nd and the clock has twenty-nine days on it, only the campus idiot needs help solving the mystery.

The new year is supposed to bring people a renewed opportunity to better themselves. So if you messed up big time during the fall semester, try not to screw up the spring, too.

New Year's Resolutions for College Kids
an observationalhumor.com classic
- Return all 37 spoons to dining hall.
- Reduce daily IM time from ten hours to nine hours. Use extra hour to play new take off of Snood.

- Remind semester abroad friends that Europe is only romantic for the first four months, and then reverts back to "non-America."
- Have a relationship that lasts at least three days, and try not to have two of them at once.
- Take down poster of Animal House guy wearing that "college" shirt. Put up poster of that ten-year-old Maxell ad where the guy's cheeks look cool.
- Stop overdrafting ATM account. Ask parents to put more money in it to help.
- Get a pair of pants that aren't black. Preferably that match new tube top.
- Set roommate's alarm clock ten minutes fast so he's only five minutes late to class.
- Create newest Napster clone instead of turning in CompSci homework.
- Make a date for Valentine's Day. Off-line.
- Call one high school friend every week. Breathe heavily and hang up when they answer the phone.
- Learn new bouncer's name so you can drop it to the next bouncer when the new bouncer gets canned in two weeks.
- Stop listening to three CDs on repeat. Get a fourth.
- Introduce yourself to page seven, row four, third from the right in the facebook.
- Duct tape front-row-seat-girl's hand down.

- Study one chapter of each subject each week. Petition Webster to swap the definitions for "study" and "ignore."

Winter Break

I bet professors look forward to winter break twice as much as we do.

When you were growing up, there was always a construction project near your house that took forever. But freshman year, your entire neighborhood was transformed by the time you got back from winter break.

Winter break is way too short for any of us to get a job. Because when most college students decide they want a job, it takes us three weeks just to get around to looking for one. By then break is almost over.

Over break, when you go to school on the West Coast but you're from the East Coast, it's very easy to convince your parents that you're up until 4:00 because of the time difference. It is a lot harder to do this when the time change is the other way around. "But mom, right now it's only 1:00. In England. See, at school, I'm studying English..."

Our parents miss us when we go to school, but they miss having us at school when we come home.

Your parents are not stupid, and they know what happens when your girlfriend or boyfriend is sleeping in your room over break. But they're OK with it. You know why? Now that you've been gone for a semester, they've been doing that, too.

Most people get bored over winter break because they forget how tough school is. There should be a day of school in January to remind us how good we have it.

Valentine's Day

I want to market candy hearts that say, "Cute or not, these taste like crap."

Valentine's Day is the loneliest day of the year for single people, yet couples totally flaunt their couplehood. I'm never a fan of PDA, but on Valentine's Day it should be a ticketable offense.

I never know how nice a gift to get someone on Valentine's Day. Keep in mind that you're going to have to beat whatever you spent when the birthday comes around.

I'm OK with taking a girl to a fancy dinner on Valentine's Day, but that means I have to pay for mine, too. While I enjoy eating a fancy dinner, it's hard enough to pay for one. And it kills the mood if I say, "Get whatever you like, honey, I had some ramen before we left, so I'm stuffed."

A parent buying their kid a Valentine's Day present should not be encouraged. If you really want to get them something, write a card that says "Happy Friday" and retain the family dignity.

Am I the only one that thinks the idea of a mostly naked toddler as the symbol of love is kind of, well, NAMBLA?

Couples going around on Valentine's Day and showing off that they have someone to date is like walking around a slum a month after winning the lottery yelling, "Yup, still rich!"

Passover & Easter

Decorating Easter eggs is a nice idea, but wouldn't it make more sense to paint something without a strictly enforced expiration date?

Since I've been old enough to know how to do it, I've always kept kosher for Passover, and I've always fasted on Yom Kippur. I figure there are 365 days in a year—I don't mind being Jewish for nine of them.

I kind of like matzah, but I will not pretend to enjoy having to eat it for eight days straight. Same thing goes for ramen noodles while I'm waiting for my loans to clear.

Chocolate eggs are a cute idea, until you really think about it. Imagine scrambled eggs. Now imagine them covered in chocolate. Still a cute idea?

If I lived somewhere and they killed me, the first thing I'd do when I was resurrected would not be stopping by the old place to say, "Hey, how's it going?"

It's no coincidence that the celebration of rejuvenation and getting a fresh start in the world comes right after midterms.

Jews don't eat leavened bread on Passover, because they hurried out of Egypt without time to let their bread rise. Which is why you should always pack at least a day before you travel anywhere. In case something goes down and everyone has to commemorate what you packed, you don't want generations of kids pissed off because you forgot to bring boxers.

Spring Break

You know why professors give you reading over spring break? Because that's when they are busy grading midterms. They know that you won't read anything until you're on the plane heading home, but the thought of it looming over you while you're on the beach makes their having to read seventy-five essays a little easier.

I understand people who go totally nuts during spring break because of the "you're only young once" ideal. I do not understand the people who go totally nuts on videotape.

The second biggest problem with spring break is that most of them come while you still can't drink legally. The biggest problem is that all of them come before you have enough money to go somewhere you can.

Some people's parents pay for their spring break, which is crazy because spring break is usually about drinking and fooling around. Then again, parents often pay for college.

People who can't remember most of their spring break still come back and say, "Man, that was awesome."

I went to Boston one spring break when it was snowing there. That's as dumb as, well, spending spring break in Boston, because nothing is that dumb.

The only thing more difficult than remembering where you put your scarf from winter to winter is remembering to go on spring break with the sunglasses you bought last year.

Summer Vacation

Some people take summer classes so they can graduate a semester early. So you're spending two summers at school when it's mostly empty and you're skipping your final semester where you have the least amount of work and the most friends. Sounds like a good deal.

The reason classes are only an hour or two long is because people have limited attention spans. During the summer, classes are usually two or three times longer than usual, which has got to make paying attention more difficult. Also, it's sunny.

I didn't go to school in California because I really look forward to summer vacation. In California, it's always summer vacation.

Why doesn't every company have internship programs? If there are hundreds of kids in every school working at summer camps for fifteen cents an hour, don't you think they'd stay around school and take minimum wage?

When you get your first 9-to-5 summer job, your alleged plans will revolve around hanging out with your friends after work and having barbecues every night with the game on in the background. Instead, you will be too tired to make dinner. And sometimes too tired to turn on the TV.

Once you hit senior year, the summer is not the summer anymore. It is the rest of the year with a little more sweat.

Other Holidays

When news of Columbus' discovery reached the Old World, everyone rejoiced and celebrated his finding: the three-day weekend.

The 4th of July is a great excuse for a date when you have access to a view of the fireworks. It's a bad excuse for a date when you only have access to a television set with a view of the fireworks.

Veteran's Day is a bit of a half-holiday. Some of America's institutions close down in celebration of the revered men and women who have served our country, and others say, "It's *what* today?"

I never really figured out what Labor Day was all about. Maybe because it happens before school starts, so it was never responsible for my drawing anything on construction paper.

Lincoln and Washington weren't born on the same day, yet some schools celebrate their birthdays as if they were. That shows that Lincoln and Washington were truly great men. Think about the skill it takes to make your birthday constantly fall on a weekend.

June doesn't really have any holidays, unless you count Flag Day. And to do that, you'd have to actually know when it was.

Some people like Thanksgiving and some people like the 4th of July. But most college guys list their favorite holiday as Father's Day. Or as we like to call it, "There But For The Grace Of God Go I Day."

Chapter 10

The End

It's been a year since I wrote *Student Body Shots*, and my perspective has changed a bit. Is it because I've graduated and have been experiencing the real world? No, I'm a writer—my only association with the "real world" is that a girl from my high school was part of the Las Vegas cast. Is it because I've been to several different campuses, and been able to see what goes on at other schools? No, because there's very little that goes on beyond a few good games of Beirut. Is it because I can no longer wake up as it's getting dark, communicate solely through Instant Messenger, and hang out with my college buddies? Are you kidding? I'm a writer—I still do all of that stuff.

My perspective has changed merely because I've gotten a year older. I visited my school after I graduated and didn't like being there that much. Sure, I missed the people, the parties, and even some professors, but I believed I was done there. I didn't experience college in some guidance counselor-mandated "right" way, but I enjoyed it. I made a heck of a lot of friends, made Dean's List as often as I missed it, (you're shocked, I know) and I had a damn good time in the process. And what's most important, I learned a lot both in and out of the classroom. See, the bar and the library are equally as important to the college education—and it's a bad sign to have a seat saved for you in either.

I found my middle ground in college, and that's the whole point of the game. Hopefully, you can find yours by the time you reach the end.

The Job Hunt

No matter how long your friends have been out of work, they are always willing to give you advice on your resume.

A friend of mine told me I was better off because I already knew what I wanted to do after graduation. But I disagreed. After graduation, I wanted to be a world-famous writer, and there aren't many classified ads for those.

Don't ever ask a graduating senior where they're working after graduation. If they don't have a job, it will piss them off. And if they do have a job, it will piss you off because you don't have a job.

Do you have a job-search friend? You can ask him anything, and he'll find a way to mention his hunt for work. "How have you been?" "Pretty good, looking for work. I'm talking to this one company." "How was your weekend?" "Awesome. I had this interview and I think it went well." "Want to head to the bar?" "Sure. You think they're hiring?"

It's tough to find an entry-level job in a bad economy because they just don't open up. Sometimes, I want to help current entry-level people find some midlevel jobs so there can be a few more spots open for the rest of us.

By the time this hits shelves, I really hope the job market is better for all the graduating seniors than it was this past year. Mainly because this book costs twelve bucks, and I need to eat.

Moving Out

When you move out, it is best to leave your posters up. Yes, you may want to take them with you, but buying new posters is easier than buying spackle.

A friend of mine vacuumed his room before he moved out. Which was very courteous, but a waste of time. With what he did to that carpet, I doubt it's staying.

If you label your boxes correctly, one of them will always be "box of random crap that didn't fit into any of my other boxes."

Now that I've graduated, I can ruin the secret: when you pack, use Kinkos boxes. They're small enough that they can't get too heavy, they've got lids so they can be closed without tape, and they're all the same size so you can stack them easily. And they're free.

Most people sell their minifridge when they graduate. This is a mistake. When you're looking at what end tables to buy for your apartment, every one of them would be more appealing if it could hold food.

People are always looking for storage space over the summer so they save on shipping their stuff home. Why don't you just rent a van and drive it there? Sure, that still costs money. But then you have stuff.

You get very nostalgic when you're moving out for the last time, and you start to think of all the great times you had at school. You look back on every fun thing you ever did. And you have time to do it at length while waiting for the elevator.

What to Ask While Looking For An Apartment—a recent grad's guide to the housing market

Note: Don't really ask any of these. Please.

Is a credit check really necessary?

Do you have a house phone, or should I just use my cell? And if I use my cell, how do I make calls between the hours or 7 A.M. and 9 P.M.?

Is it a laundry building? If so, how big a percentage of my clothing will I lose per load?

Does "cable ready" include porn?

If you include the cost of a keggerator, what do utilities usually run?

How close is the nearest public transportation that won't get me killed?

Can I get DSL? Can I get free DSL trial offers from a different company each month?

If I'm ever late with the rent, can I give you a hug and call it even?

Since I don't plan to, who is going to clean the bathroom?

Can you define "loud party?"

What if I were to accidentally put a hole in the wall the size and shape of my head. Who would fix that?

Graduation

After graduation, sell any furniture you've managed to amass. Sure, you need stuff to furnish your new place, but you can use all the money you make selling it to buy things that actually match.

Which is worse: not being able to find a graduation hat that fits you, or not being able to do the same with the robe?

There are so many parties during graduation week because everyone wants to be the one to throw the best graduation party. And everyone is entitled to try. Unless they're a junior.

When you take an extra semester or summer to finish school, they usually let you walk with your class anyway. I'm not sure I'd want to do that; that's like having to wait on the line for Space Mountain when you know you won't be tall enough for another semester.

There are a billion colors that members of the administration wear during graduation, and each color has a different meaning. Then there are the various cords, the pins, the wings, the tassels, the collars—it is way too much to keep straight. Things are less prestigious when the reaction of "Oooooh" is replaced with, "What's that one mean again?"

Honorary degrees are awesome. If I ever get really famous, I'm going to try to get a billion of them. That way when someone asks me where I got my degree, I can pull out the diploma wad and say, "The University of Everywhere."

Transition to Alumni

We go through a lot of change when we become alumni. And we use most of it to start paying off our student loans.

After you graduate, your friends will start getting married. You probably know someone who already got married while they were in college, but you're not friends with them anymore so they don't count.

I will warn you now: a few months before you graduate, start saving phone bills, credit card bills, pay stubs—anything like that. Because when you're applying for your first apartment, your landlord is going to want something better than a hearty, "Trust me."

When you get your first place, test the smoke alarms. In the real world, they don't go off every time you make french fries.

When you are on your own, you should work out a budget. Even if you don't stick to it, at least you'll know why your couch is made of old Kinkos boxes.

You only live in the real world if you pay your own electric bill and do your own laundry.

There are so many more decisions after you graduate. If you thought balancing your class schedule was tough, try getting an apartment, finding a job, and meeting the person you're going to marry. If you can't get into the right classes, you won't end up homeless, unemployed, and single. Actually, maybe that *is* the root of it.

Grad School

The main difference between being in graduate school and being in college is that while you were in college, it was OK to hit on people who were in college.

It's a lot easier to get motivated in grad school. Because in grad school you can never say, "OK, but how is this going to help me later in life?"

People in med school want to be doctors. People in law school want to be lawyers. People in graduate school for history, anthropology, or English, want to be students.

I don't understand the people who go to law school simply to put off entry into the real world. Do you know how hard and time consuming law school is? Sure, if you spend the would-be tuition money on rent and food, you won't be learning anything new. Except how to actually exist in a world outside of school.

If you think about it, most graduate schools aren't worth it. If you go to grad school straight out of college, you have one less year to work. Thus, you give up a year of your highest paid income, since you still have to start at the bottom anyway. With the exception of doctors, lawyers, and people in finance, you usually max out at $100,000. So add $30,000 in tuition to that number and you've lost $130,000. Even if grad school helps you earn $5,000 more every year for the rest of your life, you'd still have to work 26 years before you broke even—56 years if you factored in 3% inflation. Like I said, most graduate schools aren't worth it. Unless it's your parents' money. Then, totally worth it.

Choose Your Own Adventures

This can be a cold world. And I don't mean that in the sense of an it-snowed-in-South-Carolina world. I mean that the world is harsh, cruel, and generally unwelcoming to the average college graduate. Or even the above-average college graduate—you know, the guy who can locate Australia on a map.

When we graduate, we will be faced with many choices. Like the general area in which we'll live. And while we may be tempted to stay close to our schools, we should choose to move on. Otherwise, we'd have to legally change our names to "That Guy."

We could live at home, where we'll most often have access to laundry and food and cable television rent-free. Or we could strike out on our own where there's a slightly better chance of getting play.

After we decide to get our own places, we'll have to choose which relative to hit up for furniture. And then we must choose whether or not to ask why our aunts have an extra living room set.

Then there's the decision of where the furniture goes. I recommend putting the refrigerator in the living room to minimize the commute during games. And since we'll be living in the only places that we can afford on our meager salaries, we must also decide which corner of the hallway to call our living room.

The biggest choice is a job. Fortunately, that choice is not left solely up to people who just graduated college, since we'd all be torn between a Nobel Prize, bartending, and figuring out how to win a Nobel Prize for bartending. If breaking up a drunken brawl isn't peace keeping, I don't know what is.

The people with whom we choose to interview make our job choice for us. Sure, we also choose whether or not to shower that morning, but beyond that it's out of our hands. And it's not even always our choice to apply for the job. Sometimes, the company is simply run by the friends of our parents.

The jobs for which we apply usually come in two forms: those that we've been dreaming of our whole lives, and those that come with paychecks. I guess graduate school is a third option, but if we choose that, we're just adding a few years to our ages before having to go back and make these choices anyway. Going to graduate school is like taking a different path in a Choose Your Own Adventure book. We may learn a little bit more about our destinations, but we'll either cycle back to where we were or get eaten by the two-headed monster at the end (Debt and Unemployment—stay with me here).

And though the dream job might be wonderful, that's only if you get it. Searching for jobs online while eating cereal for dinner is not so wonderful. If you want to quit your lucrative finance job to pursue your doctorate in order to become a professor, well, if that's what you want to do, then go for it. If you want to quit your high-paying finance job to pursue your singing career through American Idol, I'd advise against it. What I'm saying is that we should all pursue our dreams. Except when our dreams are stupid.

Trainspotting said to choose life, which is silly since I don't know many people who would choose otherwise. Our choice is really *which* life, and we all have to remember that our choices are not always made consciously or even willingly. But whatever we do choose, we need to make sure it keeps us warm. Like I said, this can be a very cold world.

Especially while sitting near a refrigerator.

Special Features

"It's special because it's featured."

Steve's Inserts and What Not

Five Instant Away Messages 23
I Know This Kid Who Did This Thing 61
Page 69 69
Dear Mr. Bouncer 72
What to Ask While Looking For an Apartment . . 100
Choose Your Own Adventures 104

Steve's Classic Observational Humor

The Definition of Drink 43
New Year's Resolutions For College Kids 89

"What? You're still here? It's over. Go home."